CONDITIONING
FOR ATHLETES

CONDITIONING
FOR ATHLETES

Michael A. Winch

Foreword by Emeka Udechuku

THE CROWOOD PRESS

First published in 2005 by
The Crowood Press Ltd
Ramsbury, Marlborough
Wiltshire SN8 2HR

www.crowood.com

British Library Cataloguing-in-Publication Data
A catalogue record for this book is available from the British Library.

ISBN 1 86126 744 4

All photographs are by the author, except where otherwise credited.

Disclaimer
Please note that the author and the publisher of this book do not accept any responsibility whatsoever for any error or omission, nor any loss, injury, damage, adverse outcome or liability suffered as a result of the information contained in this book, or reliance upon it. Since conditioning exercises can be dangerous and could involve physical activities that are too strenuous for some individuals to engage safely, it is essential that a doctor be consulted before undertaking training.

Typeset by
Florence Production Ltd
Stoodleigh, Devon

Printed and bound in
Great Britain by
Biddles Ltd, King's Lynn

CONTENTS

Foreword

As a discus thrower I have always been aware of the necessity of being able not only to throw, but also to run, to jump and to 'work out' in the gymnasium. The discus thrower must be more than proficient in all the athletic disciplines, and conditioning is of fundamental importance in this event.

When I was young I took part in sprinting, jumping and throwing at school, and this laid the foundations for my later success as a discus thrower. However, when I took part in major championships the stakes were raised, and increasingly I had to concentrate on conditioning in order to achieve success.

The cold evenings in winter when my coach, Mike Winch, insisted that the group run 800m as a time trial, are firmly ingrained in my memory, as is the track and gym work that we endured over many months and years. Nonetheless, this was essential preparation that enabled me to compete successfully at the highest level of the sport.

Conditioning is often considered to be a complex subject, and many athletes do not want to know the details; they just want to train and improve. Naturally, for the coach it is completely different. He or she must take into consideration the individual needs of the athlete, and must employ many different and interesting methods in order to help the athlete achieve improvements in performance. Without an extensive knowledge of conditioning techniques, the coach will never be able to train the athlete successfully; and without utilizing all the available options, the athlete will never achieve his or her ultimate potential.

Mike Winch's *Conditioning for Athletes* is an invaluable book that contains something for every athlete and coach, from athletes at the very start of their career, to experienced coaches looking for something new. It is all covered in these pages, and I can strongly recommend this book to all those involved in athletics at whatever level.

Emeka Udechuku
Olympian, 2004, Athens

Preface

This book is the companion volume to *Strength Training for Athletes*, also published by The Crowood Press, and it contains a mass of information on conditioning for the coach and athlete. It also has over 300 pictures to help you understand the techniques described, and will be a constant aid to improving the training of athletes at all levels. It is simple to follow and yet detailed enough to be of worth.

There are many ways to improve an athlete's results, but, without the foundation of basic conditioning, no athlete will be able to reach the pinnacle of performance that is the reward of good training. This book will help, although it does not pretend to have all the answers. It will, however, offer the coach and athlete a wide range of activities to add to, or form the basis of, future learning.

The exercises contained in the text are all of proven worth, and the structured schedule that they follow has a long history of success.

Enjoy this book, and use it to add to your knowledge and expertise.

Michael A. Winch
2005

Acknowledgements

This book has been produced during a very stressful period in my life, and it is only with the constant support of, in particular, Carole, my wife, that it has been completed.

Thanks must also go to Judy Oakes OBE, who features in a number of the photographs and who has also pushed me along the route to finishing.

Maggie Lynes, Abdul Buhari and Anthony Soalla-Bell, three of my athletes, worked hard as models for many of the exercises, for which I cannot thank them enough.

Finally, I would like to thank my mum, who, as a writer herself, has long suggested that I should put pen to paper.

Introduction

'Conditioning' is the most important word in the athlete's vocabulary: it is the essence of athletic performance and survival in the heat of competition and, without it, athletic lives are short and never reach the heights promised by their potential.

But what exactly is meant by 'conditioning'? Most people are comfortable with a general definition such as 'being fit enough to train and compete', but this really only describes the very early stages in athletic skills. As the athletic endeavour becomes more specialized and the rigours of training and competing become more intense, so too should the extent and intensity of the conditioning work.

Conditioning is the preparation work that enables the athlete to train and compete. Clearly, this will be different for the endurance runner, the high jumper and the javelin thrower, and is therefore specific in nature. But this specificity is really no more than a difference in the balance of the same basic fundamentals, with a certain amount of event-specific conditioning when required in the later stages of an athletic career.

The physical elements that make up a conditioning programme must therefore be appreciated for their individual benefit, and then applied in differing balance according to the skill required, to provide the specific accent required for the specific event. These elements are mobility and suppleness, core stability, aerobic and anaerobic conditioning, speed and power, general strength and event-specific conditioning, and are discussed below.

Take, for example, a long-distance endurance runner. The events have a very high aerobic content, a smaller anaerobic content, and need very little strength but high core stability. The range of movement is limited and the skill is minimal. Clearly, then, the balance of the conditioning work needed must be heavily biased towards the ability to sustain activity for a long period of time economically, employing a correct and stable technique. Excess muscle bulk gained from heavy weight training and power sprints would largely be a waste of time, and counterproductive in achieving the desired goal. Nevertheless, there needs to be a proportion of speed and strength conditioning to keep the body optimally balanced for accelerations during the race, and possibly at the finish should a sprint be necessary to win.

Contrast this with the shot-putter, who needs little aerobic or long-term anaerobic

Fig 1. Endurance athlete.

capacity, but massive strength, both general and specific, explosive speed and a large range of movement. The balance of the elements of conditioning for this athlete would therefore be totally different from that of the endurance runner, but, in parallel to the former example, the shot-putter also needs aerobic and anaerobic conditioning in order to train hard enough to improve the other elements.

The key, therefore, to conditioning is to establish and put into practice the elements

Fig 2. Shot-putter.

needed to produce the very best results in the event for which the athlete is training. In this way the effectiveness of the time allocated to each segment of training will be maximized, and useless or minimally productive work eliminated, as nearly as possible, from the programme.

Often athletes train extremely hard and produce very little by way of results; a situation that is not only very depressing for the athlete, but also the coach. The application of logic and of sound scientific principles to conditioning is therefore essential to make the progress of any athlete not only satisfying, but also rewarding to both the participant and the trainer. This is particularly relevant to young athletes, who can often be overspecialized, ending up on the scrap heap of sport before they should even have been thinking about focusing on a single event. We have all seen youngsters being thrashed around tracks and in gymnasia, performing work more suited to an aspiring Olympian. These are the potential athletes who are very often lost to the sport: they have glory days when their peers are not even thinking about serious training, and then end up being swallowed up in the group as they reach true training age.

This is not to say that youngsters should not be allowed to train, but that appropriate and wide-ranging conditioning should be applied to give them the best chance, not only of choosing the right event, but also of having a happy and fulfilling athletic career. The word 'appropriate' is most importantly applied to the design of the conditioning programme. Without the controlling influence of appropriateness, the programme will have little relevance either to the athlete or the event that he or she is trying to advance in.

As a guide, young athletes from eleven to fifteen years old should be exposed to all events, and should follow a more general conditioning programme so they can experience each individual skill with a measure of satisfaction. From fifteen to eighteen years old they should move to event group specialization and conditioning, and from then to their chosen event and its specific conditioning training. This progress is much slower than we normally see, but it will lead to an excellent grounding in the basics, before event specificity narrows the focus too much.

Some of the best examples of bad practice include the use of hurdle jumping to condition the legs for plyometric ability. Because the hurdles can only be lowered to a set height, this is often used as the starting point for athletes, regardless of whether they can actually jump that high or have enough eccentric leg strength to stop them collapsing when they land. The solution is simple: make them jump over very low obstacles until they can cope, or start them off with hurdle stepping until they are sufficiently conditioned to start jumping. Similarly, bad practice can often be seen in the use of resistance running, such as tyre pulling, in the sprints. If the force is too great, excessive stress is placed on the Achilles tendons, which will inevitably become injured. Simply using the *appropriate* level of resistance will avoid such problems, and if in doubt this should be absolutely minimal.

It cannot be stressed too strongly that despite the coaches' and athletes' enthusiasm to reach the top as soon as possible, great care and patience must be applied to guarantee eventual success. There is not a single Olympic champion who has not done his or her apprenticeship over many years, repeatedly modifying and improving the training programme to the point where a breakthrough to the highest level has been achieved.

Years of appropriate conditioning work can lay the foundation of success; years of inappropriate conditioning can only lead to frustration and failure. The conditioning programme gives the athlete the ability to achieve, and without it there is no platform from which to improve.

SUMMARY

Conditioning is the work needed by the athlete to prepare for the stresses and strains

Fig 3. Hurdle jumping.

of eventual specific training and competition. It consists of a number of separate and distinct elements relating to the needs of the event. These elements need to be applied in a carefully constructed programme, and in an appropriately balanced ratio for the best results. Bad practice will lead to bad results, and even injury.

The conditioning programme must be an integral part of the whole regime, and must reflect the individual needs and age of the athlete as well as the event. When correctly designed and applied, conditioning will not only produce the best results in terms of competition, but also prolong the life of the athlete within the sport.

CHAPTER 1

The Physical Elements of Conditioning

The table below charts the basic elements of conditioning training.

All the physical elements of conditioning are separate and distinct, defined by their physiological nature. The starting point in learning how to build a conditioning programme must therefore be an understanding of the events themselves. It is often the case that the coach's knowledge is not broad enough to appreciate, and therefore define, the fundamentals of an event, and thus determine its component conditioning parts. As a first stage in this process we will therefore look at all the elements, and explain what they are, and how they are relevant to athletic events.

The elements are mobility and suppleness, core stability, aerobic, long- and short-term anaerobic, speed and power (including plyometrics), general strength and event-specific conditioning.

	Joint Mobility	Suppleness	Core Stability	Aerobic	Long-term Anaerobic	Short-term Anaerobic	Speed-power	Plyo-metrics	General Strength	Specific Strength
ACTIVITIES	Active mobilizing	Active suppling	Medicine ball work	Long-distance steady running/ walking	Interval running	Sprints (including up and down hill)	Sprints (including up and down hill)	Low/high box jumping	Weight (general exercises)	Weight training and multi-gym work (specific exercises)
	Passive mobilizing	Passive suppling	Fixed position resistance activities	Fartlek	Fast short-distance running	Speed endurance running	Bounding/ hopping	Bounding/ hopping	Multi-gym training	Heavy implement training (throws)
		PNF suppling	Body-weight mid-region, back and leg work	Faster shorter-distance steady running	Uphill/ resistance running	Uphill/ resistance running	Fast event skill movements	Hurdle jumping	Isokinetic training	Event movements against resistance (resistance running)
			Resistance mid-region, back and leg work	Circuit training	Speed endurance running	Power sessions	Power sessions	Flat ground reactive jumping	Body-weight training	Body-weight training
			Swiss ball mid-region and back work	Stage training (light weights – body-weight)	Circuit training	Maximum-speed weight training (45% maximum lift)	Maximum-speed weight training (45% maximum lift)	Multigym plyometrics		
					Stage training (light weights – body-weight)	Light fast weight training (20–30% maximim)				

MOBILIZING AND SUPPLING

Mobility is the range of movement allowed by the joints. Suppleness is the range of movement allowed by the muscle-tendon soft tissue structures. They are therefore distinct and separate. Mobility conditioning is needed to ensure that each joint has maximal range of movement. Athletes generally start off their careers with a full range in all joints; however, as they progress there is a tendency for this to be lost as more and more training is performed without the accompanying maintenance of mobility. It is essential therefore to retain joint mobility as part of the overall programme.

Suppling is also a necessary aspect of everyday conditioning. As the muscles and tendons are worked over the years there is a tendency for them to shorten, thus reducing the range of effective movement. This is best illustrated by the throwers, who must attempt to reconcile heavy weight training over a limited range with projecting implements over as long a distance as possible. The heaviest weight training tends to shorten the muscles and tendons by virtue of the relatively small ranges of movement used; therefore the athlete must ensure that extra suppling training is performed to counteract this. The historic term 'muscle-bound' reflects this problem.

Athletes should therefore be encouraged to work on both mobility and suppleness as a major and consistent part of their conditioning programme.

CORE STABILITY

The term 'core stability' has recently been used to focus on the problems relating to obtaining and maintaining correct posture during athletic performance. Good conditioning of the muscles of the spine, sides, abdomen, hips, ankles and the other stabilized areas of the body is most important if the athlete is to be able to perform correct and balanced movements of the limbs. If these muscles are not efficient and effective,

Fig 4. Massive muscles of the thrower.

Fig 5. Long jumper demonstrating firm body position.

then it is impossible for the limbs to carry out the sophisticated techniques required in athletic events.

The aspect of core stability conditioning which makes it different from all-round body conditioning is that the muscles involved in stabilizing the core of the body do so by working isometrically (non-moving); they thus hold their contractions in fixed positions for considerable lengths of time, and so may be considered to be operating from an endurance base.

The design and operation of the core stability conditioning must therefore take this into consideration. For example, after the start and acceleration, the sprinter must maintain his/her body position in a near-erect position while the legs and arms produce the movement over the ground. During a 400m run, therefore, the stabilizing muscles hold the spine in an erect position by working near-isometrically for the duration of the race. This would indicate that the exercises need to be performed in such a way as to equate to this, perhaps by holding a fixed position for up to 60 sec or longer.

Anyone who has tried this will realize just how tiring it is, and how hard you must work to achieve sustaining the contraction for that long. Nevertheless, recent work has suggested that such activities greatly benefit the athlete, and reduce the development and occurrence of back, hip, knee and ankle problems.

Core stability conditioning is therefore an essential part of any athlete's programme, and needs to be a separate and clearly defined element of that programme.

AEROBIC CONDITIONING

As the name suggests, aerobic conditioning improves the ability of the athlete to operate physically for long periods of time, normally without an external resistance, moving just the bodyweight. It involves the intake of oxygen, and the 'burning' (oxidation) of a balance of carbohydrate and fatty fuels within the muscle cells to produce the high-energy compound used for muscle contraction, adenosine tri-phosphate (ATP), and the waste products, water and carbon dioxide.

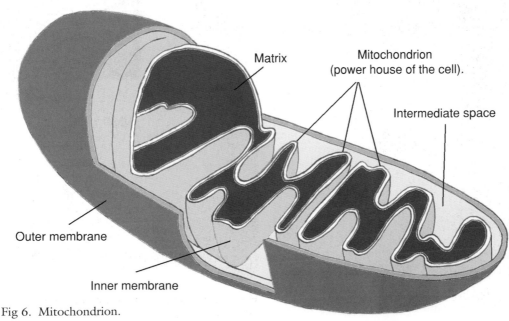

Fig 6. Mitochondrion.

This oxidative process is called glycolysis, and it occurs in and around the mito-chondria – very small, oval objects found in abundance in slow-twitch (aerobic) muscle fibres, and to a lesser extent in fast-twitch (anaerobic) fibres. It involves many complex biochemical reactions that are controlled by enzymes – proteins that accelerate and moderate all chemical reactions within living tissue.

Aerobic ability relies to some extent on the levels and efficiency of these reactions, but also on the levels of oxygen and the fuel substances (glucose and fatty acids) that are oxidized during the reactions. It therefore also depends on the efficiency of breathing, the ability to take in oxygen and exhale carbon dioxide, and the ability to circulate the blood to the lungs and the appropriate muscles.

Improvement in the aerobic ability of an athlete is controlled by the body's adaptation to aerobic stresses put on these systems, and is therefore highly complex. The most basic form of aerobic conditioning is therefore any exercise that makes the athlete's pulse and breathing rate increase moderately and sus-tainably, as during steady running, cycling, rowing and walking, or some of the more recent machine-based activities such as the cross-trainer.

There has always been argument and scientific research into what improves aero-bic capacity the most. Regimes including long slow runs, faster shorter runs, Fartlek training and mixed sessions have all been advocated and proved successful. More recently the use of a low-oxygen environ-ment to stimulate natural Erythropoetin (EPO) production has come into vogue, since it lifts the red blood cell count and therefore the oxygen-carrying capacity of the blood.

At a basic level, however, running or walking at a steady pace are the best and sim-plest ways of stressing the body's aerobic systems and increasing their efficiency. This is applicable to all athletes, even the throw-ers. These generally heavy athletes mostly shun such activity as they find it very arduous, not only because of their bulk, but also because they usually have a high level of fast-twitch anaerobic fibres within their muscles, and consequently little aerobic capacity.

The proportion of aerobic conditioning that is needed by each event depends on the level of aerobic activity within that event. For example, the long-distance runner at one extreme might spend upwards of 90 per cent of training time on such activities, whereas the shot-putter might only spend 5 to 10 per cent of training time. This huge difference is determined by the needs of the event and also the physiological problem that fast fibres can be converted to slow ones, but not vice versa. Thus an explosive, fast athlete could reduce his or her speed capacity by perform-ing too much aerobic conditioning work. So far there is little evidence to suggest that this process can be reversed.

Long- and Short-term Anaerobic Conditioning

The word anaerobic means 'without air' and indicates the nature of this activity. It is based on the production of energy (in the form of adenosine tri-phosphate) in the muscle by processes that do not use oxygen as a main chemical precursor. The energy is produced in several ways:

- the oxidation of carbohydrate-related products to produce lactic acid;
- the conversion of creatine phosphate (CP) and adenosine di-phosphate (ADP) to cre-atine (C) and adenosine tri-phosphate (ATP);
- and the conversion of two molecules of ADP to form one of adenosine mono-phosphate (AMP) and one of ATP.

All of these processes take place inside the muscle fibres and are controlled, as with the aerobic activity, by enzymes. The processes themselves are much more rapid than the aerobic reactions, and therefore result in quicker contractions of the muscles and hence bodily movements.

The different ways of producing energy anaerobically in the muscles relate to two different types of fast-twitch muscle fibre: one used predominantly in slightly sub-maximal contraction speeds, as in the 200m and 400m races, and the other during maximal speed activities in explosive events such as the shot put. These are respectively known as long- and short-term anaerobic activities.

Long-term anaerobic activities mainly employ the formation ATP, the high-energy chemical that directly causes muscle contraction, accompanied by the production of the by-product, lactic acid. Such activities can be maintained at the highest speed over a period of time up to 45–50sec. The problem with this type of energy production is that the by-product, lactic acid, is very poisonous to muscle activity being strongly acidic. Every athlete who has run 400m as fast as possible will recognize the symptoms of high lactic

Fig 7. Sprinting to win.

acid levels in the muscles: pain and rapidly decreasing efficiency of movement.

Anaerobic conditioning for the type of event that produces lactic acid on a large scale needs to address two distinct problems: first, the efficiency of the biochemical pathways that create energy by the production of lactic acid; and, second, the removal of the lactic acid from muscle during and after its production. The conditioning normally used to enhance these two functions is based on producing and sustaining high levels of lactic acid during the activity, which should be simple in nature. Examples of this might be a session of running 150m without allowing full recovery between repetitions. Alternatively, circuit training or body-weight stage training in the gym would have similar effects on the body, but in a less specific way.

Short-term anaerobic activities utilize the formation of ATP directly from the breakdown of two molecules of ADP to one of ATP and one of AMP. Alternatively, molecules of CP and ADP are converted into ATP and C. This is a rapid progress, but can only last for around 8–10sec or less, which is why the 100m sprinter slows over the last stages of the race. Conditioning for this includes work that enhances the stores of creatine phosphate and its efficiency of breakdown; basically anything that stresses the muscles over a short period of time at maximal or very near maximal speed.

SPEED AND POWER

Conditioning for the explosive athlete needs to be focused on repetitive activities involving maximum- or near maximum-speed movements; these can include sprint starts, bounding and weight exercises. These all contain an element of plyometric movement, which cannot be divorced from any maximum-speed activity, but is nevertheless an individual conditioning element. Flat-out movement depends on high-speed muscle contraction and on the levels of creatine phosphate in the muscle, and its ability to produce ATP; hence the recent focus on creatine levels in the muscle and the extensive use of creatine supplementation among present-day athletes. Caution, however, must be observed in the use of this substance in the diet, as high and even moderate levels can cause cramp during activity, with resultant injuries.

It is thought that absolute top-speed muscular movements lasting only fractions of a second are based on small reserves of the prime high-energy compound (ATP) within the muscle fibres. Such stores are extremely small, and thus true maximal speed can only be maintained for very short periods of time. Conditioning for such fast movements must involve true maximum-speed activities, such as plyometrics and maximum-speed non-resistance movements.

Interestingly, absolute maximum-speed ability can only be improved by a small percentage above the athlete's natural level, since it is determined by the genetic make-up of the muscle fibres, and there is little evidence that the proportion of fast fibres can be increased. However, an athlete's speed of movement can be increased dramatically by skill (neuro-muscular co-ordination) and strength conditioning, basically because any movement involves the resistance exerted by the bodyweight, strength and skill being

Fig 8. Explosive delivery of the thrower.

needed to overcome it. This is really the difference between speed and power. An athlete might be very fast, but too weak to use this speed during an activity. Building strength increases power (power = speed × strength) and consequently such training can turn a potentially fast athlete into an actively fast one.

This is particularly relevant in relation to youngsters, who might appear to be slow simply because their strength has not kept pace with their developing stature. The conditioning of young athletes must take this into consideration, general activities being much more important at this stage than specific ones as the body's structure develops and changes.

Most explosive events require the athlete to be powerful *in comparison with* their bodyweight. There would be no point at all in gaining strength while considerably increasing muscle bulk, since this would be creating a decreasing strength-for-weight ratio, and performance would therefore be reduced despite the strength gain. In most events, the target must therefore be to create little or no bodyweight gain while increasing strength. This does not, of course, apply to the heavy throwers, who actually gain in performance from increased muscle bulk – though even *they* must be careful that the ratio does not decrease too far. There are several tests that can be applied to check on this, one of which is the standing long jump. In general terms, the longer the distance jumped, the higher is the strength-for-weight ratio.

Recent work has indicated that the elasticity of the tendons is largely responsible for reactive or plyometric ability. For example, it would seem that, during the phase in a sprint where the runner reacts to ground contact, the calf muscles maintain an isometric (non-moving) contraction, while the Achilles tendon produces the movement in the ankle by acting like an elastic band being stretched and then recoiling. This points up the importance of reactive conditioning for events requiring a quick and powerful reaction to the feet landing on the ground.

Fig 9. Long-jump take-off.

Other elements of this ability include an efficient co-ordination of the stretch reflex and conscious muscle contraction during extended reactive movements, as well as sufficient specific strength to perform the movements.

All of these abilities are best improved using plyometrics, which is the general name given to reactive conditioning training, and includes hurdle jumping, bounding, hopping, depth jumping, box jumping and other related activities.

Because of the explosive and stressful nature of plyometrics, only short sessions are used, because tiredness can lead to injury.

In addition, tiredness soon reduces the reactive response and therefore makes the activity of decreasing value. Young athletes and beginners must start with low-level work, and only when they have a thorough background of basic plyometric conditioning should they progress to a slowly developing programme of more robust and stressful activities. Progress that is too rapid usually leads to problems, for instance 'shin splints' – a common result of inappropriate levels of plyometric training.

CIRCUIT AND BODYWEIGHT STAGE TRAINING

These basic forms of exercising have been used for many years as the nucleus of any conditioning programme as used by most athletes. Circuit training involves performing a series of exercises in a set sequence, and then repeating the sequence two or more times. The fact that an exercise is performed only once per circuit means that the whole body becomes fatigued during the session, rather than individual muscle groups. Thus circuit training results in good aerobic and long-term anaerobic adaptation by the athlete.

Stage training is completed by performing one exercise the required number of times, with a short rest in between sets, and then moving on to the next exercise. Thus all repetitions and sets of each exercise are completed before the next is started. This is different from circuit training, as the specific muscles used are fatigued and then not used heavily again, unless deliberately as part of the session design. Stage training therefore improves the local muscular endurance of the muscles used in each exercise.

These two forms of conditioning are easy, versatile and good fun to perform, and can be used at all times of the year to develop and improve the aerobic, anaerobic and local muscular endurance abilities of the athlete.

GENERAL AND SPECIFIC STRENGTH

These activities are covered in the companion book, *Strength Training for Athletes*, published by The Crowood Press. Suffice it to say here that all athletes need a basic grounding in strength training to maximize their performance, and each event can benefit from specific strength training to properly enhance the muscles needed to perform the movements correctly.

Some time will be spent in later chapters on the very basic elements of strength training as well as some more specific methods used, either as part of a particular part of conditioning such as core stability, or as elements of a programme specifically to improve an event, or part of an event.

SUMMARY

Conditioning represents all the basic elements that need to be in place if the athlete is to progress safely and efficiently to his, or her, potential. Without proper and effective conditioning work, training will become ineffective, and sometimes even counterproductive. The conditioning work must be closely integrated into the overall programme.

The young athlete needs to work on all conditioning elements equally, while the more mature athlete will tend to focus on a more event-specific programme.

All of the conditioning elements have a clear purpose, and involve a spread of relevant activities. The coach must be aware of, and understand, the extensive range that is at his or her disposal. In this way the training programme will produce the best results.

CHAPTER 2
Mobility and Suppling

For athletic events, movement is produced by the muscles applying force using the bones as levers, the joints being the pivot points or fulcra. Each joint, be it elbow or knee, has a finite or maximum range of movement for the individual concerned, some lesser and some greater. This maximal range of movement is called the 'full mobility' of that joint. Normal range only approaches this full range when there are no restrictions to movement, such as large muscles or injuries. It is vital, therefore, that any athlete retains, or even extends, their normal range of movement to as close to full mobility as they can for their specific event.

Some coaches believe that no more than sufficient range of movement is necessary to satisfy event needs, whereas others feel that near maximal range is safer in order to avoid short- and long-term injuries, and to optimize performance. Both theories have been applied, and both have produced world-class results, but intuitively it seems right to keep all the joints at maximum functional efficiency, if only to protect against the unexpected that sometimes requires greater range movements than the event itself.

As athletes train, they invariably increase muscle tone and bulk, even if the overall size seems not to change. Such improvements to the muscles do paradoxically create resistance to movement; young athletes in particular tend to become very unsupple as a result. The joints themselves are not restrictive, but the increased muscle tone and size cause this reduced suppleness, and, unless this is corrected, it will cause a deterioration in the range of applying force, and therefore reduced performance. The problems that are noticed most often occur in the hamstrings of runners, who work very hard on those particular muscles, and yet still manage to injure them. In many instances this is caused by the hip flexors being tight, thus forcing the hamstrings to work too hard as they pull the leg back in the running action.

Mobility and suppleness are therefore related, but are not the same, and the coach must be able to ascertain where any problems lie. Two illustrations of this will show up potential problems: first, a simple exercise to test for calf/Achilles tendon suppleness is for the athlete to squat as low as possible with the head up and the back held straight, as near upright as possible. An acceptable suppleness will allow the athlete to reach a position with the top of the thighs parallel with the ground, and the feet firmly flat; if there is restricted range of ankle flexion, the heels will lift the athlete on to the toes as he or she squats down. The problem can have two main causes: one is the suppleness of the calf/Achilles tendon; the other is that the ankle joints do not have sufficient natural mobility to allow the required flexion. The former can be corrected, but the latter cannot. It is surprising how many athletes have restricted ankle mobility, and it is important to pick this up early, because forcing the joint to flex by continued suppling can in fact damage it, as well as straining the calf and tendons.

The second example is the throwing-arm shoulder joint of the javelin thrower, who must have great range of movement to allow the correct throwing action. As the thrower gains strength, so the joints are held more tightly together, and the range is reduced. However, certain athletes have restricted mobility simply by virtue of their shoulder-joint structure, and can never achieve the great range of movement needed to become world class. In this event, elbow joint mobility is another factor in determining eventual success. Javelin throwers are born, not created. Nevertheless, all javelin throwers must work hard to maintain, and if possible increase, the range of movement within the shoulder in order to enjoy maximum range of delivery.

Some athletes simply cannot achieve the necessary range of movement for an event, and understanding this is just as important as realizing that some simply do not work hard enough to achieve that range. The coach must be aware of which it is and, if the problem cannot be resolved, professional advice should be sought.

LOOSENING AND SUPPLING

Suppling should not be confused with the loosening that needs to be performed before training and competition. Suppling should be performed away from such situations, as it is very stressful to the muscle/tendon units and if practised correctly will reduce elasticity and muscular response for a considerable time.

It is therefore important that loosening, rather than suppling, is performed before training and competition. Loosening is defined as working to between 90 and 100 per cent comfortable range. Suppling, by comparison, would be from 100 per cent to beyond comfortable range. In addition, loosening should involve event-specific active or dynamic movements, rather than the more commonly used static non-specific suppling. This has the additional useful effect of bringing the body to an active state by stimulating the neuro-muscular relevant pathways to the event.

Many coaches do not distinguish between the two, with the result that overstretched athletes compete, and then end up injured. This is most common for sprinters, who like to feel loose hamstrings but often damage them before they even reach the track.

CORE STABILITY AND SUPPLENESS

Core stability problems are often associated with weakness in the muscles of the mid-region, and a lack of suppleness. Often the latter causes the former, because, if the range of movement is small, the muscles cannot be strengthened over their full range, with the inevitable consequences of incorrect normal passive posture and poor stability, as well the inability to maintain correct posture during exercise.

By analysing the event and the movements it entails, the coach can assess the needs of the athlete, and correct any imbalances that exist. This is an important feature of the

Fig 10. Athletes warming up with loosening.

training plan, as effective range of movement and the stability of the body core, which allows the limbs to operate over that range, is a fundamental of all athletics.

Muscle Tone

One other factor that influences range of movement is muscle tone, or the state of readiness of the muscle to contract. Athletes vary in their normal level of tone, and it should be a target to increase muscle as far as possible. Some athletes, however, have the problem that when they start intense physical activity their muscles tighten, thus reducing range of movement and creating a potential injury problem when maximum range is attempted. This can be overcome with appropriate mental training for relaxation, an aspect of the programme that needs specialist advice and consultation.

Interestingly, creatine supplementation increases muscle tone significantly, which is why many athletes are cramping more when taking it. The use of creatine has to be monitored very carefully, and it should be noted that those athletes with high normal muscle tone are most severely affected by this problem.

METHODS OF SUPPLING

There are basically three methods of stretching or suppling, each requiring care and precision. These are:

- Passive
- Dynamic
- PNF (proprioceptive neuro-muscular facilitation)

The passive method is to perform the movement slowly, reaching the final point and holding it for a number of seconds before relaxing. Such slow movements prevent the stretch reflexes from activating and causing a sudden contraction which potentially could cause serious injury. This is the most commonly used method, and the simplest.

Fig 11. Suppleness of the hurdler.

The dynamic approach is often spurned as being potentially injurious, and indeed it can be if performed without care and attention. The method involves moving into positions of stretch dynamically so that the momentum of the movement overcomes any stretch reflex and extends the tendon/muscle unit accordingly. If performed too fast the unit can be damaged, but if performed with care it produces very effective results. This has been particularly well demonstrated by British gymnasts who have recently been employing Russian coaches. These highly skilled trainers had no compunction in using extreme dynamic stretching as a major part of their work, much to the surprise of British coaches who had largely avoided such work.

PNF stretching involves the reduction of the stretch reflex (and thus the natural resistance to lengthening a muscle) by contracting the muscle statically prior to stretching. This has proved to be a very effective method. It is best actioned with two athletes

Fig 12. PNF hamstring stretch.

working together, one to resist the contraction and apply the stretch, and the other being stretched. The contraction should be strong and held for around 6sec. This is then followed by the stretch in the opposite direction, which is again held for another 6secs. This is repeated six times, on each occasion the range being pushed that little bit further.

It is surprising just how quickly suppleness can be improved using this method, which is probably the quickest and most direct method to increase the range of movement. It is, however, very tiring, and should not be attempted close to any form of maximum output training.

BASIC SUPPLING EXERCISES

Ideally athletes should supple for at least twenty minutes per day, and should use a logical approach to how the session is performed. A simple sequence of exercises is the most effective and balanced way of proceeding: starting with the neck and working systematically down the body ensures that all

necessary areas are covered in the session; it is also easy to remember.

The following are examples of basic suppling exercises: most exercises are best performed five or six times each, with a 6sec hold at the final position where applicable, followed by a 10–15sec rest between stretches. This will create effective adaptation within the tendon/muscle unit, but without causing damage.

Neck stretch: It is very important not to overstretch the neck as the vertebrae are small and easily damaged by over-vigorous

Figs 13, 14 & 15. Neck stretch.

flexion. Actions to avoid are extreme backwards movements of the head, as these have a tendency to compress the vertebral spines, with obvious deleterious effects; and sideways stretches, although these tend to be less potentially damaging. The forward range is safe, and very useful in stretching not only the muscles of the neck but also the nerves emanating from the spine.

The neck stretches should be performed slowly and carefully and never beyond the range of pain. Athletes often wake up with a 'cricked' neck after cramping during sleep, and these should always be treated with great care, and never eased by forced movement. Massage is far more effective than stretching in easing the symptoms and returning neck mobility to normal.

Isolated shoulder rotation: The athlete should slowly rotate both the shoulders forwards and backwards, using the trapezius, upper back and pectoral muscles to produce

an exaggerated rotation. As with the arm rotations, it is important to use both shoulders simultaneously, as this ensures that the movement is not assisted by body rotation, and also that a better stretch can be applied.

Shoulder and arm rotation: The classic shoulder and arm suppling exercise: use both arms simultaneously while holding a Cliniband, rope or stick to maintain a constant distance between the arms. Using a nonelastic implement is better because progress in increasing the suppleness of the shoulders can be measured by how close together the hands can be placed while still smoothly working the rotations.

Shoulder forward and backward stretch: The athlete should move both the arms simultaneously forwards across the body at shoulder level using the pectorals, and then backwards behind the shoulders at the same level by activating the rhomboid and

Figs 16 & 17. Isolated shoulder rotation.

Figs 18, 19 & 20. Shoulder and arm rotation.

Figs 21 & 22. Shoulder forward and backward stretch.

Fig 23. Standing side stretch.

Figs 24, 25 & 26. Standing mid-region rotation.

posterior deltoid muscles. The movement should be performed slowly and precisely, and held at the extreme ends of the ranges for about 6sec. The arms must be held in such a way as to avoid the shoulder joints dropping and rotating, thereby making the movement easier.

Standing side stretch: Often the sideways movement of the body is inadequately carried out, which means there is little improvement in the suppleness of the muscles involved. It is best performed by leaning to one side and simultaneously taking the opposite arm extended above the head and reaching it over towards the bending side, at the same time fixing the body to prevent the hips from moving sideways and aiding the movement. This produces a very effective stretch along the full range of each side.

Standing mid-region rotation: The standing mid-region rotation is a general exercise that can be used to stretch the muscles involved in this particular movement. The athlete should stand with the feet wide apart in a sideways split to fix the hips in position, and then rotate the shoulders slowly round to one side as far as possible; hold that position for about 6sec before rotating to the other side, and again holding. Take care to keep the movement steady and evenly balanced, although there may be some difference in range between the two sides.

Lying spinal curve stretch (forward flexion): It is important to keep the full length of the spine supple, and this exercise will help to achieve this. The flexing version requires the athlete to lie on the back and take the legs over the head to as close to the ground as possible. Curvature can be

Figs 27 & 28. Lying spinal curve stretch (forward flexion).

Fig 29. Spinal curve stretch (backward extension).

Figs 30 & 31. Seated hamstring stretch.

increased by bending the knees and trying to touch them, rather than the toes, on the ground. The final position should be held for about 6sec. Some lateral stretch can be applied by walking the toes, when on the ground, to either side.

Spinal curve stretch (backward extension): This movement must be performed with great care, as too great a hyperextension of the back can impact the vertebral spines. The safest way is to lie back over a large inflatable ball (Swiss ball) so that the stretch can be released simply by rolling sideways. The object of the stretch is to relax the muscles and stretch over the ball with the arms and legs extended. This position should be held, as with most of the other exercises, for about 6sec. If pain occurs during this exercise, it should be investigated before continuing, as it may indicate a weakness or injury in the area.

Seated hamstring stretch: The seated hamstring stretch is the easiest controllable hamstring stretch exercise. It is performed by sitting on the ground with the body held erect. From here the arms are extended horizontally to prevent the back rounding, with the head held up and facing forwards. The abdomen is then pushed forwards towards the feet. Additionally, the toes may be pulled back towards the body as the stretch is progressed. Hold the stretched

position for about 6sec before relaxing back to the start position. This is repeated on the other leg.

Standing hamstring stretch (free and leg supported): This is a frequently used exercise for improving hamstring suppleness, but it is less controllable than the seated version. In the 'free' version, stand up straight with the legs locked, and gently lower the body forwards until the hands reach the ground. The more supple athletes will be able to do this comfortably, in which case to stretch the hamstrings effectively they must flex the arms and push the forearms to the ground. It is advisable not to bounce up and down vigorously, but rather to move slowly and purposefully.

The 'leg supported' version of the exercise is performed by standing and resting the leg to be stretched on top of something of comfortable height, such as a hurdle or wall. The body is then pressed towards the thigh, as in the seated version, so that the hamstrings and gluteals are stretched. Care must be taken not to curve the back over as this gives a false impression of the actual suppleness. The final position is held – as with the other exercises – for about 6sec.

Lying hip flexor stretch: One of the most important advances in the understanding of athletic performance has come with the realization that the hip flexors are a very

Figs 34 & 35. Standing hamstring stretch (leg supported).

Figs 32 & 33. Standing hamstring stretch (free).

Fig 36. Lying hip flexor stretch.

Figs 39 & 40. Standing adductor stretch.

Figs 37 & 38. Split-leg hip flexor stretch.

Figs 43 & 44. Kneeling quadriceps stretch.

Figs 41 & 42. Standing abductor stretch.

important part not only of leg movement but also basic core stability. It has become clear that many back problems originate with a lack of suppleness in this area. One of the best exercises to improve this is the lying hip flexor stretch, best performed with two people. The person to be stretched lies on a physiotherapy bench or its equivalent with one buttock on and one off, and the body lying along the bench. The leg to be stretched is then lowered, extended, towards the ground, while the lower back is held flat on the bench and the non-active leg is held bent up to 90 degrees with the foot held firm on the bench. The helper controls and stabilizes the movement. Gravity provides the stretching force, but in cases of great stiffness, the weight of the leg may be partially taken by the helper and the movement assisted with controlled downward pressure.

Split-leg hip flexor stretch: This exercise is also very effective in stretching the hip flexors, and can be performed without the aid of a bench or helper. The athlete kneels on one knee, pushing the other foot well forward into a wide split position, and placing the hands behind the back. From here, he pushes the hips forwards while keeping the shoulders back: this will give an arching position, and the hip flexor will be stretched over the hip. The final position is held for 6sec before relaxation. It is very important that the hips are forward and not rotated, otherwise the lower back takes the strain.

Standing adductor stretch: The adductors can be stretched simply by placing the legs well astride, while bending forwards towards the ground. When the maximum sideways split is achieved the athlete then gently stands up, thus applying a stretch to the adductors. This exercise must be performed carefully and slowly, and the final position held for the usual 6sec.

Standing abductor stretch: This is performed by standing sideways on and holding on to a wall bar or other fixture, with the abductor to be stretched on the outside. The legs are then crossed, with the leg that is to be stretched placed in front of the other. The body is then carefully and slowly bent away from the foot of the stretch leg, thus forming a sideways curve with the body and a stretch on the abductor. This position is held for 6sec, and the movement repeated after a 10–15sec rest. Both sides are worked.

Standing and kneeling quadriceps stretch: Suppleness in the quadriceps is most important for all athletic events, but is often neglected. The standing stretch is performed by standing on one leg, grasping the ankle of the leg to be stretched behind the back, and pulling it up and back away from the buttocks. The final position is held for 6sec, and the leg then relaxed. It is important to create an arched position in order to stretch the muscles effectively; when performed in this way, it has the additional useful effect of working the hip flexors at the same time. Because of the large muscle bulk of the quadriceps, considerable work is needed in order to make any progress, and up to ten stretches can be performed without deleterious effect.

A more controlled stretch for the beginner or less experienced athlete is the kneeling version of this exercise. It is performed by kneeling on the ground with the hands behind the feet and touching the ground. From here, the body is arched back supported by the arms, and the hips are pushed forwards. This stretches both the quadriceps and also the hip flexors, and is therefore a controllable and effective exercise for these two muscle groups, which often have too little attention spent on them.

Seated and standing calf stretch: The calf/Achilles tendon units are very susceptible to injury and, since the feet are the primary contact points with the ground and therefore the main force application points in all events, it is vital that the associated soft tissues have maximum suppleness. There are a number of simple exercises that can be used, and one of the most controllable and effective is the seated stretch. The athlete sits on the

Figs 45 & 46. Standing calf stretch.

ground with the legs out straight and together. The balls of the feet are then grasped firmly and the toes pulled steadily towards the body, the final position being held for the usual length of time. The toes are then pointed forwards for a short rest, and then pulled back again. It is important to relax the calves during the movement to avoid invoking the stretch reflex. The ability to perform this assumes good suppleness in the hamstrings and gluteals.

The calves can also be stretched in a controlled manner by leaning forwards with the arms outstretched and the hands resting on a wall. One foot is then taken back with the leg straight, to the point where the heel comes about 10cm off the ground, while the other leg remains forward and flexed, supporting the body. The body is then steadily pushed back, at the same time relaxing the stretched calf and trying to push the heel down to the ground. If the heel is able to touch the ground the foot is moved further back for the next repetition. After holding the final position for 6sec the pressure is released for about 10sec, and the movement repeated.

EVENT SPECIFICS

Each event has its specific requirements for suppleness, but largely these are extensions of the basics rather than anything additional.

Running, Hurdling and Walking

Running in general requires little more than general suppling. Hurdling requires the range of movement to be greater in the hips (sideways) and the lower back (forwards) and associated muscles. Walking is a little different in that the range of movement of the ankles (calf/Achilles units) and hips when the legs are straight must be maximized. Specific suppleness in those areas and under the restrictions of the event are paramount. In all running and walking events, athletes tend to focus on the lower body, but it is essential that all regions are properly suppled to ensure that maximum force can be efficiently applied through a relaxed full range, and correct posture maintained during the completion of training and in the course of competition.

Jumping

The jumping events often entail extreme ranges of movement: for example, in the high jump the free knee is driven upwards as high as possible and the back is arched as part of the flow over the bar; likewise, the triple jump requires maximal stretch fore and aft between the legs, particularly during the step phase. It is therefore vital that suppleness is maximized in the specific muscle/tendon units specifically relating to the events. It is the unbalanced or incorrect movement that needs the safety net of full mobility and excellent suppleness, and it is often because these are inadequate that it ends in injury.

The best advice is, therefore, to encourage the athlete to work hard on suppling to reduce the risk of injury, and to enhance the ease with which the technical skills of the events can be performed.

Throwing

Often the heavy throwers are the least supple of all the athletes, perhaps with the exception of the javelin experts, who must work very hard on shoulder, hips and mid-region suppleness just to perform the movements involved with reasonable efficiency. The problem is usually that the muscular bulk gained in heavy weight training leads to a reduction in movement range because it physically obstructs the joint and therefore its ability to flex. This is often compounded by

a lack of suppling work, with the result that, despite good strength increases, performance fails to improve. It is therefore essential that suppleness is a major part of the thrower's training programme: it must not be sacrificed on the altar of greatly enhanced strength and muscle bulk.

SUMMARY

Every athlete must maintain and if possible enhance their suppleness in order to ensure maximum technical skill and range of applying force. Rarely does joint mobility present a problem: it is more often the stiffness and shortness of the muscle/tendon unit that creates difficulties. Suppling should be performed carefully and precisely to produce the most beneficial effects. Short daily routines are effective, and should be separate from technical or high-level training sessions, because suppling, when performed correctly, inherently causes muscle/tendon fatigue. Before hard training or competition, active loosening, and not suppling, should be employed to enhance performance and reduce injuries.

Core stability is often adversely affected by a lack of suppleness, and training must therefore include both elements to be beneficial. If a good, all-round general suppling routine is in place, little extra specific work is required, except where specific technical requirements demand it.

CHAPTER 3
Core Stability

Core stability has recently been the 'buzz phrase' in sport conditioning, a term used to describe the stability needed for the proper functioning of the body's most basic activities: sitting, standing, walking and running properly. Without this simple ability it is impossible to perform with any skill or accuracy the more difficult movements in athletics and other sports. Furthermore, in addition to the improved ability to perform skills, there is the protective effect of core stability training: the lower back is one of the areas of the body that is most susceptible to injury, and core stability conditioning helps to protect that vulnerable region as well as the connected musculature, such as hamstrings, adductors and hip flexors, that is so important in bodily posture and movement.

It is surprising to find that many athletes cannot perform even the simplest of activities with correct posture, a failing that in many instances can be attributed to a lack of physical activity earlier in life, or because they have never been taught how to move correctly. Increasingly, we see more and more children without even a basic ability in

Fig 47. International star Tony Jarrett demonstrates posture in hurdling.

running, jumping and throwing, and it is these who must be conditioned very carefully to improve their basic core stability.

If this happens at an early age a steady progress can be maintained as they move on to more complex movements; but unless this physical work has been well integrated into their everyday life even the most talented athletes cannot improve much without injury.

WHAT IS THE BODY CORE?

Simply explained, the legs are connected to the upper body by the spine. The spine is held in position by many muscles, all of which connect the two main areas of the body together. These include the muscles that hold the spine itself in position, as well as the tube of muscles that stretches from the spine around the front of the body and basically holds the abdominal contents in place. This tube of muscles is the focus of most athletes' abdominal work – but the other stabilizing muscles that run internally from the spine to the legs, and others running up and down the back, are just as important.

This is one reason why the old term 'abdominal exercise' now forms only a part of the whole core stability muscle training. An understanding of how the core muscles work and are co-ordinated with movement has now been developed so that the athlete can maximize the effectiveness of his or her training by exercising in the best way.

A simple example of this can be seen in the way the athlete stands. The old deportment-class activity of walking with a book balanced on the head would actually be difficult for many athletes, as they do not consider that walking upright has anything to do with their sport. It is, however, surprisingly relevant, as only when this postural position is correct do the muscles that operate the limbs work most effectively.

Runners often suffer from tight hip flexors because either they do little effective stretching on them, or the muscles are weak and over time have become rigid. As a con-sequence of this the hips tilt forwards, and it is difficult, if not impossible, to lift the knees up to any degree without curving the lower back at the same time. This naturally would lead to great difficulty in sprinting or running fast.

The resolution to this lies in two activities: first, sufficient stretching to ensure full range of movement; and, second, sufficient strength training to ensure that the hip flexors are strong enough not only to lift the knees, but to help hold the hips in the correct postural position during exercise. This com-bination of flexibility and core muscle strengthening is a vital part of all athletes' training, and must be a focal point for the coach's conditioning programme.

Suppling has been dealt with in the previous chapter. We will concentrate here specifically on aspects of core stability muscle strengthening that are not covered else-where.

CORE STABILITY MUSCLE STRENGTHENING

This type of strengthening is performed in a manner different to that for the muscles that move the limbs. The reason is that, to produce stability, the muscles operate in a near isometric way: that is, they contract, but do not produce movement, a little like the guy ropes that support a tent. In addi-tion to the isometric contraction there is the time factor to be considered, namely the length of time they remain contracted. An understanding of these principles under-scores the methods developed for strength-ening these muscles specifically in relation to the way the exercises are performed, and the length of time the contractions involved are maintained.

Take as a simple example a guardsman standing to attention for several hours: the product of such an activity – or apparent lack of activity – is, perhaps surprisingly, intense fatigue, particularly in the lower back, and it is only by the constant practice of standing still that the fatigue diminishes and the soldier is able to remain comfortably on

Fig 48. Press-up start position.

guard. It is clear to anyone who has tried this kind of activity that you need to be very fit and strong in the core stabilizing muscles, and have considerable endurance ability in those areas, simply to stand upright for any length of time. Athletes not only need to stand, but also to perform intense physical movements without the body's core section moving out of place.

This, then, leads us to an understanding that the core stability training should incorporate sufficiently lengthy contractions to ensure that the muscles can operate over the required time-span of the event. In modern-day competition this does not just mean the time it takes to perform the event, it also includes warm-up and the lengthy procedure of waiting your turn to compete. A marathon runner needs to be able to maintain good postural position for over two hours in the race and for a short time before setting off. A long jumper or discus thrower performs for much less time in active mode, but the competition itself can last as long as a marathon, and tiredness must not set in during that period. Both, therefore, must

train the muscles in a similar manner to ensure that fatigue will not degrade his or her performance up to, and for the duration of, the competition.

There are a number of ways to produce the desired effect. These include bodyweight, weight and other resistance, medicine ball and Swiss ball conditioning. Specifically for core stability, each of these activities must be performed in a similar manner to ensure that the positions attempted can be maintained for increasing lengths of time. This is the essential difference between most other forms of conditioning and core stability work.

Isometric Muscle Contraction

As we have seen above, when a muscle is contracted in a static position it is called an isometric contraction; certainly historically it has been used as a means of increasing muscle size and strength. In the 1950s Charles Atlas promoted its use commercially for improving the physique, but since then further work has shown that isometrics only strengthens the muscles over a very narrow range outside the static position adopted. The strengthening effect extends to about 15 degrees of range either side, indicating that such exercise would be of little use in strengthening muscles to produce movement. It does, however, suggest that isometric contractions could be very important in strengthening core stability muscles in a way similar to that in which they operate normally.

This is in fact the case, since these muscles are more concerned with holding fixed postural positions than creating movement. This, then, defines the way in which core stability activities must be performed.

Take the simple press-up as an example. This exercise requires the athlete to hold the body in a horizontal position supported by the arms and feet. The arms are then bent so that the body lowers to the ground, and are then extended to raise it to the initial position. Simple enough, but consider what the core mid-region muscles must do when the body is lowered and then raised: they must fix the whole body in a straight line, and, if a set of twenty press-ups is performed, this may involve a period of up to a minute. Since no movement of the mid-region is required, the core stability muscles are acting isometrically for the whole time. Athletes with poor core stability will have difficulty doing this, and will wobble and sag during the movements, and this is a clear indication that more conditioning is needed in the mid-region area.

To improve the athlete's ability to perform press-ups well, it is clear that the body core needs considerable isometric strength endurance work to enable him or her to sustain the correct postural position.

BODYWEIGHT EXERCISES

Core stability bodyweight exercises include any exercise that uses only the athlete's bodyweight and is performed isometrically. Examples of such conditioning are as follows, although this list is by no means comprehensive. The coach should use his or her imagination to invent and apply a range of

activities, since by definition the work is hard and fairly boring to perform. A range of sessions makes the work more bearable, and keeps the athlete focused.

Each exercise is performed for a defined period of time, followed by a period of rest; initially this should be 30sec hold and 30sec recovery, and this is repeated four times for each exercise. Each week the 'hold' time is increased by 10sec up to a maximum of 1½min, after which a new exercise should be introduced having a similar effect. The recovery time is kept at 30sec. Where the exercise uses one leg or arm at a time, four sets are performed on each side to ensure the maintenance of balanced development.

The other important factor in such work is to ensure that correct posture is used in all exercises. This means that sufficient suppleness of the soft tissue and mobility of the joints must be a precursor to working on core stability. If an athlete is too stiff to achieve good neutral positions, then there is no way that the more difficult core stability exercises should be attempted.

Below are some examples of exercises, but the coach can invent new ones or modify the old to have the effect needed.

Press-up position: This is performed by adopting the initial press-up position (Figure 48).

Press-up position reverse leg raise: The same starting position is adopted, and then one leg is raised above horizontal to the rear, and held there.

Press-up position leg and arm raise: The same position is taken up as for 'press-up position reverse leg raise' above, but in this case one arm and the opposite leg are raised and held in position.

Standing knee raise: The athlete stands on one leg, the arms held out horizontally in front or to the sides, with one knee raised so that the top of the thigh is parallel with the ground. This must be performed with the hips held in the same position as for standing on two legs, the lower back not being

Figs 49 & 50.
Press-up position
reverse leg raise.

Fig 51.
Press-up position leg and arm raise.

Figs 52 & 53. Standing knee raise.

allowed to curve outwards as the knee is raised.

Standing outward rotated knee raise: This is performed as in 'standing knee raise' above, except that the knee is rotated outwards to as near 90 degrees to the natural position as possible.

Standing inward rotated knee raise: This is performed as in 'standing knee raise' above, except that the knee is rotated inwards and up towards the stomach.

Standing inclined leg raise: The athlete stands on one leg, hands held out horizontally in front or to the sides, and carefully leans back about 30 degrees at the same time raising one leg (held straight) to the front at the same angle, to keep the body and raised leg in a line. This should not be performed by athletes with lower back problems.

'T' position: Again, the athlete stands on one leg; then lowering the body forwards and lifting one leg simultaneously, he or she attains a 'T' position with the body and leg horizontal. There must be no twisting of the supporting leg. The arms are stretched out to the side.

Lying hip raise: This is performed by lying on the ground with the hands by the sides. From here the hips are raised off the ground. This is easier to perform if the legs are very slightly bent and the weight is taken on the heels and shoulders. Keep the head and neck relaxed to avoid strain.

Lying abductor raise: The athlete lies on his or her side with the body and legs in a straight line. The head is rested on the ground-side arm, and the other arm is bent and the hand can be rested on the ground for stability. From here the higher leg is raised to about 45 degrees (or higher if possible), keeping it in line with the body. There should be no rotation of the hip, and the foot should remain parallel with the ground.

Free crunch, double- and single-leg: This is a simple and basic central abdominal muscle exercise. The athlete lies on his or her back, and forces the lower back on to the ground by tensing the abdominal muscles. The legs are then raised slightly off the ground and the head and shoulders lifted slightly so that the abdominal muscles tighten further. This position is held for 3sec, and the head and feet then relaxed back to the ground.

Figs 54, 55 & 56. Standing outward rotated knee raise.

Figs 57, 58 & 59. Standing inward rotated knee raise.

Figs 60 & 61. Standing inclined leg raise.

Figs 62 & 63. 'T' position.

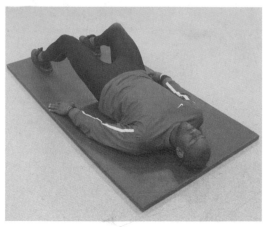
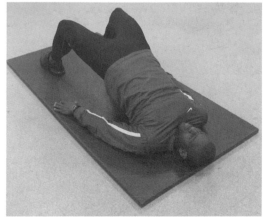

Figs 64 & 65. Lying hip raise.

Figs 66 & 67. Lying abductor raise.

Figs 68, 69 & 70. Free crunch, double- and single-leg.

This can be performed with either both feet raised to the same height (double-leg version), or one leg higher than the other (single-leg version).

WEIGHT TRAINING AND OTHER RESISTANCE EXERCISES

The use of weights and other resistances adds to the difficulty in performing the exercises, but their best use is in activities where the body is held in a fixed position while the weight or resistance is moved around this position. The exercises are therefore not performed as in the other core stability work, since a static position cannot be held while the implement is being retrieved and the initial position regained. In addition the resistance applies considerable stress, and the positions are difficult to maintain for lengthy periods. These exercises are therefore performed as sets of a small number of repetitions (for example, six sets of three).

Sandbag Throwing

This activity used by throwers involves a bag full of sand with straps attached near each end. This is held in two hands, and the body is fixed in the throwing delivery position. From here the bag is thrown forwards, while strictly maintaining the body's position. The heavy weight applies a strong force, which has a tendency to move the body; the core stability muscles must therefore work hard to prevent this.

Fig 71. Strict back squat body position, in mid-lift.

The bag can be thrown from various event-specific postures, as well as being used in simple activities such as walking or standing in various positions.

This is an excellent way of forcing the core to adapt to the strong forces that occur during the field events, particularly the throws.

Basic Weight Training

Basic weight training has a high core stability conditioning element. For example, the simple back squat requires the athlete to fix the body position while the legs are flexed and then straightened. Since the weight is on the shoulders, considerable strain is created along the full length of the back. Because the effort seems to be in working the legs, the effect on the core is often ignored. Any athlete who performs squats for the first time, however, or after a lay-off, well knows which muscles it works . . .!

All weight exercises when properly performed require considerable core stability, and in truth, if performed technically well and strictly in position, a properly balanced weights programme will give the athlete most of the core strength he or she needs. This is not to say that other core work is wasted, but, rather, that there are always areas of weakness that weight training will not specifically help. It is to address these that other work is needed, most often event-specific stability training.

Isometric Weight Training

This is an often ignored form of training that can have very considerable benefits. It is usually utilized only by experienced athletes, as performing the exercises requires a knowledge and experience of heavy weight training.

Isometric weight training sounds like a paradox, since weight training is usually defined in terms of movements. Isometric weight training, however, is defined in terms of positions. If we again consider the back squat, the isometric version entails the athlete attaining and holding in the usual core stability pattern, a static position that is part of the normal movement. Positions can vary from a shallow to a full knee bend, and any position in between. Holding any of these for 30sec or more is extremely hard, since the core muscles are forced to operate strongly to maintain a good posture. Similarly with the bench press: even though the athlete is in a lying position, the body has to be held firm to perform the exercise well.

Many variations can be used to work a point or a position of weakness. This makes isometric weight training a very versatile adjunct to the arsenal of activities relating to core stability conditioning.

MEDICINE BALL EXERCISES

The medicine ball is another useful tool in developing core stability. Because of its varied resistance it can be used for young and weak athletes as well as the more experienced. On the whole, it is used in a manner similar to the sandbag, as the athlete can move the medicine ball while maintaining fixed postural positions. Its main area of use is in event-specific work, although there are many straightforward activities that can be a fun way of training the core without the boredom of simple static work.

With imagination, a whole range of exercises can be developed and used in varied sessions, again giving the coach the option of being able to offer interesting and enjoyable diversions from the grind of ordinary training. Group as well as individual work can be used to help team spirit and harmony within the squad. (Chapter 10 is devoted to describing and explaining a range of basic exercises.)

SWISS BALL EXERCISES

The Swiss ball is the most recent of implements to be incorporated into the athlete's training programme. The ball has been used for many years in diverse activities such as Pilates, remedial therapy and related forms of exercise. It provides the athlete with an enjoyable yet hard form of training which

Figs 74 & 75. Lying single-leg raise.

Figs 72 & 73. Seated single-leg raise.

can be adapted to use in both general and specific core stability work. As with the other core stability activities, there is a wide range of exercises that can be used, thus making Swiss ball sessions interesting as well as fruitful.

Below are some basic exercises, but remember that these are only a sample of what you can develop into a useful library of activities to ensure that athletes are strong enough in the mid-region to perform their chosen event.

Seated single-leg raise: The athlete sits firmly on the Swiss ball with the body verti-

cal and the arms outstretched, with the legs at 90 degrees, and the lower leg vertical. From here, the athlete moves slowly forwards until nearly falling off the ball, the feet being adjusted so that they are again at 90 degrees' bend. One leg is then raised to the horizontal and held in position for the required time. It is then returned to the starting position, and the other leg is raised.

Lying single-leg raise: In this exercise the shoulders are rested on the ball with the body outstretched, the arms held away from the body and the legs at 90 degrees. It is important that the body is held very firm and in line

Figs 76, 77 & 78. Lying sideways move.

Figs 79 & 80. Single-arm raise with body in press-up position.

Fig 83. Kneeling double-arm raise.

Figs 81 & 82. Kneeling single-arm raise.

Figs 84 & 85. Kneeling single-arm/leg raise.

with the upper legs. From here, one leg is straightened to the horizontal and held there. When the requisite time has elapsed, the starting position is regained and the other leg lifted.

Lying sideways move: The starting position is the same for the 'lying single-leg raise' exercise, above. From here the shoulders are pushed to one side, keeping the upper body horizontal rather than twisting it. Once the most extreme position has been attained it is held for the required time before moving to the other side of the ball.

Single-arm raise with body in press-up position: For this exercise the feet are placed on the Swiss ball, and a press-up position is adopted with a firmly maintained, straight body; from here, one arm is raised in line with the body and held in position. After holding for the set time, return it to the ground, and then raise the other arm.

Kneeling single-arm raise: This exercise requires great skill. The athlete kneels on the ball with both hands also resting on it. When stable, one arm is raised to the hori-

zontal. This is then repeated for the other arm. The difficulty is with balancing, which of course is more difficult for the weaker athletes.

Kneeling double-arm raise: This requires great stability to perform. The athlete kneels on the ball with the body vertical and the arms down by the sides. From here, both arms are raised to the sides and held in position.

Kneeling single-arm/leg raise: The starting position is the same as for 'kneeling single-arm raise' above. From the start position, one arm and the opposite leg are raised to the horizontal and held there for the required time. After this the starting position is regained, and the opposite leg and arm are raised.

Feet raised crunch: This is a simple and effective exercise. The athlete lies on the ground face up, and places his or her feet on the ball with the legs at 90 degrees bend or holds them freely in the air at the same angle. The shoulders and head are then lifted off the ground and that position held for the set time.

Figs 86 & 87. Feet raised crunch.

Figs 88 & 89. Feet raised, arms outstretched crunch.

Feet raised, arms outstretched crunch: This is similar to 'feet raised crunches' above, except that the arms are held above the head for the duration.

Variations on these exercises can be performed while standing on the Swiss ball, but this requires great skill and balance and should not be attempted by beginners or those with a fragile nature. It is wise to perform such exercises on a soft surface, since even the best athletes will occasionally fall off the ball.

Kneeling and standing on the Swiss ball can be a starting point for some very advanced and effective event-specific work, particularly for the throwers. These athletes can use these initial balancing positions to practise throwing movements with and without implements, but, as stated earlier, do not expect beginners to be able to perform this type of work easily. It takes great skill and perseverance to reach a stage where any movement at all can be performed while balancing on the ball.

The Swiss ball is, in my view, a major new asset in the library of core stability conditioning techniques, and it can be used by all athletes at some level regardless of ability.

They are cheap to purchase and simple to use – though, as always, skill is the prerequisite for effective usage.

SUMMARY

'Core' means 'centre' or 'heart'. 'Core stability' is therefore the centre or heart of stability, or the means by which the body holds its posture. If the muscles involved in this continuous process are weak or lack endurance, the athlete can only approximate the position he or she needs to perform well.

Core stability conditioning can be achieved using a wide range of methods, all of which require hard work and perseverance. Because of the wide variety of activities, core stability training can be made fun and interesting. However, only limited progress will be attained if the same activities are repeated endlessly.

Once competence has been achieved, it will be that much easier to perform the highly skilled movements required in athletics and, of course, most other sports. Add to this the protection that a strong core gives, and the overall benefits of such conditioning are clear.

CHAPTER 4
Aerobic Conditioning

Aerobic exercise is defined as that involving the cellular combustion (burning or oxidation) of carbohydrate and other energy sources, using oxygen. In addition to energy in the form of the high-energy reactive biochemical adenosine tri-phosphate (ATP), carbon dioxide and water are the products. Hence during aerobic exercise significantly increased carbon dioxide levels are found both in the blood and in the outward breaths. Internally there are both simple and complex physical and biochemical processes.

The simplified equation for utilizing glucose to produce energy aerobically is as follows:

$$Glucose + Oxygen >>>>> Carbon\ Dioxide$$
$$+ C_6H_{12}O_6\quad 6O_2 \qquad\qquad 6CO_2$$

$$Water + ENERGY$$
$$6H_2O \quad\ Adenosine$$
$$Tri\text{-}phosphate$$
$$(ATP)$$

There are many steps in this process, all mediated by enzymes, co-enzymes and vitamins. Essentially it is a three-stage process: glycolysis – the breakdown of glucose into simpler compounds; Krebs' cycle – the breakdown of these simpler compounds to carbon dioxide and water utilizing oxygen; and ion transfer – the formation of the usable high energy compound ATP. It is unnecessary for the coach to know these in detail: the most significant practical factors are the importance of glucose, oxygen and B-vitamins in this process.

Aerobic exercise is the most efficient activity in terms of energy consumption. A 100m sprint consumes around 25 kilo-calories per 100m, whereas a 1,500m run consumes only 11.3 calories over the same distance. The difference, of course, is the speed of the activity, and it relates to the different muscle fibres used in each. The faster event almost exclusively uses fast-twitch fibres whose energy is derived anaerobically, a less efficient method of energy production. The longer run uses mainly the slow-twitch fibres which use energy mainly produced aerobically and therefore more efficiently.

Breathing itself is the basis of aerobic exercise. The mouth, nose, throat and lungs all play their part in the efficient intake of oxygen and output of waste products, as of course do the muscles and nerves which create the physical action that expands and contracts the ribcage. These physical processes are mainly controlled by centres in the brain stem (the *medulla oblongata*), but can be overridden by conscious mental effort.

Within the lungs, the intricate network of ever-smaller branches of the air passages culminates in the delicate alveoli (air sacs) in which the exchange of gases take place. Oxygen crosses over into the blood from the inhaled air, and carbon dioxide passes from the blood to the exhaled air. This process is mediated by diffusion gradients across the blood–alveoli cellular barrier, a process that requires a moist lining to the lungs. This is why it is often difficult to run continuously in very dry air.

Once the oxygen has passed into the blood it is carried first by the heart and general circulation to the muscles, and then by way of tiny blood vessels called capillaries close to the muscle fibres themselves. Here, the oxygen passes into the fibres, and carbon dioxide passes out by the same process as in the lungs.

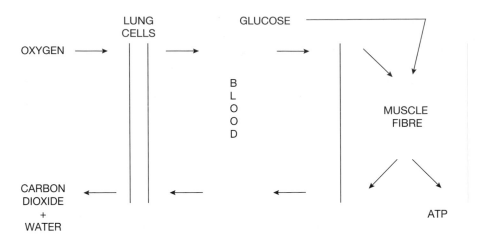

Simple view of aerobic energy production

Fig 90. Long-distance runners.

Once in the muscle tissue the oxygen becomes involved in a complex series of biochemical reactions that result in the formation of the high-energy compound called adenosine tri-phosphate (ATP), together with the waste products carbon dioxide and water. When not used, ATP reacts with creatine to form some creatine phosphate, the high-energy compound used to store a certain amount of readily available energy that is involved in producing the initial burst of contraction in fast-twitch fibres. Thus oxygen does influence fast movements, if only indirectly.

In aerobic exercise the oxygen intake is sufficient to produce enough energy to sustain continuous activity. In addition to the carbohydrates that are burnt, fatty acids derived from fats are also utilized, and the balance of the two changes the longer the exercise continues. It is thought that 'the wall' in marathon running is connected to a major switch in basic food sources for the aerobic energy production system, possibly when there is no more readily available carbohydrate, which causes a switch to the burning of fatty acids.

Also involved in this whole process at cellular level are certain vitamins of the B group. These highly water-soluble vitamins must be readily available if the process is to progress at maximum efficiency. From this it can be seen that, although aerobic exercise is the simplest form that can be enjoyed by all people, it is nevertheless highly complex, employing physical, chemical and dietary elements, all combining to produce a simple result.

All athletic events involve some proportion of aerobic energy production, and it should therefore be at the heart of all athletic preparation training. Without good basic aerobic conditioning, no athlete can train or perform at their highest peak; it is therefore essential for some level of aerobic training to be part of all training programmes. Basically, such training is simple, particularly in events where aerobic fitness is not the main objective of the event as it is in the endurance events.

IMPROVING BASIC AEROBIC FITNESS

To improve aerobic fitness involves increasing the supply of oxygen to the muscles, the availability of carbohydrate, and the efficiency of the various biochemical reactions. These adaptations are stimulated by performing medium-level exercise for extended periods of time. The exercise is surprisingly specific in that cycling, while it improves the basic aerobic fitness level, does not do much for running, and vice versa. Training must therefore reflect as closely as possible the specificity of the activity for best results.

Having said this, to most athletes, running for extended periods is boring and should be interspersed with other activities, such as cycling, rowing, cross-trainer and power walking. A mixture is much easier to sustain than a steady grind with little interest. In addition, the alternative exercise forms are significantly less damaging to the joints, particularly for the heavy event athletes.

Extensive research has been conducted on aerobic fitness and the basics are well known. These suggest that the best way to improve is to train within pulse rate limits, which vary with age. The diagram below defines those limits.

Along the bottom axis (x-axis) the age is plotted, and along the vertical axis (y-axis)

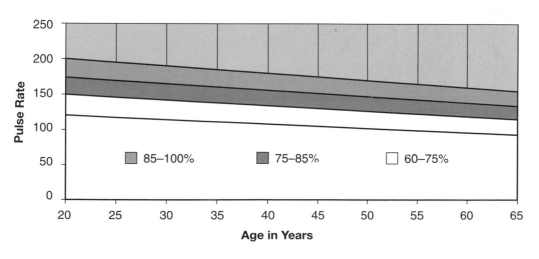

Training ranges by age

the training pulse rate is plotted. The top band represents the 85–100 per cent training range, the middle band the 75–85 per cent range, and the bottom the 60–75 per cent range: these represent the anaerobic training range, the high aerobic range and the low aerobic range.

Exercising with the pulse rate in the high aerobic range gives the best results for improving the aerobic fitness level, but initially the lower band should be used to start the process of adaptation. A minimum of twelve minutes' continuous exercise is sufficient to stimulate aerobic adaptation, but this should be extended as the fitness increases. It must be remembered, however, that there is evidence that fast-twitch muscle fibres can be converted into slower aerobic fibres if the pressure to adapt aerobically is too great. Only sufficient aerobic conditioning should therefore be used to allow the athlete to train for the specific event efficiently.

TESTING AEROBIC FITNESS

There are a number of tests for aerobic fitness, but most are designed to measure the levels accurately and are therefore time-consuming and have little bearing on the needs of the majority of athletes. Perhaps the best known of these is to measure the VO2 max which is the maximum oxygen uptake per minute. It reflects the oxygen used during exercise but does not measure the comparative efficiencies of the various processes of aerobic energy production. The simplest accurate version of this test still requires the volume of breathed air to be measured, together with the percentage of oxygen in the exhaled air. This of course can only be done in laboratory conditions, which in the main do not perfectly reflect natural road or track running. The test however is worth conducting once a year if possible to assess the aerobic fitness against 'norm' tables. Generally, however, non-endurance athletes would not need to perform it more often than this, if at all.

A better simple test for these athletes is simply to perform a standard distance run

such as an 800 or 1,500m: this will give an excellent indication of aerobic fitness, since all athletes, including the heavy event exponents, should be able to complete such a task without too much stress.

Winter or inclement weather can necessitate the use of a simple gym-based test. One of the best is simply to run on a treadmill for five minutes bringing the pulse up to around one hundred and eighty beats per minute, taking the pulse at the end and then every minute for five minutes. The drop in pulse rate should be to below 100 beats per minute after 90 to 120sec to indicate a good level of aerobic fitness. Any longer indicates insufficient aerobic ability, pointing to the need for increased training effort in this aspect of the programme. Interestingly, this simple test also anticipates illness, as the heart rate tends to stay high in such circumstances. It can also be used to assess recovery from illness, and is a good indicator of overtraining, which seems to relate closely to the body's response to illness.

ADDITIONAL AEROBIC CONDITIONING METHODS

Circuit training: This method has been used for many years as a serious and effective way of improving aerobic fitness while introducing different muscles into the session. A full explanation and sample sessions are found in Chapter 7.

Stage training: Stage training using light weights or just bodyweight improves aerobic fitness, but is more focused on local muscular endurance than circuits. Chapter 8 covers this type of conditioning.

Mixed sessions (running, jumping and skills): Combining running, jumping and skill work is a most effective and interesting way to promote aerobic fitness, and can be used to break the monotony of long, steady aerobic sessions. This type of conditioning is useful for all athletic events, and sessions can be devised both in the gym and also at the track. It is important to remember that jumping ability declines rapidly with fatigue, as does skill, so nothing too difficult must be introduced into the session for risk of injury.

Combinations of short runs, low jumps and skill manoeuvres can be combined into a 15–30min session depending on the requirements of the athletes. There are an infinite number of variations and combinations that can be used, so that each session can bring a refreshing newness to the programme.

ADDITIONAL BENEFITS OF AEROBIC TRAINING

Aerobic conditioning has a number of very beneficial effects to all athletes. These effects are, of course, the same for the general public, but, since the athlete must have as full a control over all aspects of the body as possible, these ancillary outcomes are of greater significance.

Blood Pressure and Heart Rate Control

High blood pressure is one of the factors contributing to heart disease, and this affects athletes as well as everyone else. Aerobic conditioning helps to reduce blood pressure and thus the stress on the heart. It does so by stimulating the formation of capillaries throughout the body, and thus by improving the supply of oxygen and nutrients to the tissues. In addition it helps to keep the arteries in top condition, and the heart rate below the norm. It must be said, however, that for some individuals these effects will not be enough to protect them from heart disease, as other factors are overriding. Nevertheless, as a general rule the effects of such training are very beneficial as regards keeping the blood pressure below normal levels.

Weight Control

The plague of obesity that is now so evident in all sectors of the population, and particularly in children, is a direct result of the massive reduction in physical activity in all groups of the population. In addition the poor food quality of modern life exacerbates the problem. Fortunately it is now accepted that exercise, and particularly aerobic exercise, should be part of a long-term bodyweight and body fat control. This is because, if some aerobic work is performed daily, the metabolic rate increases and the digestion, assimilation and utilization of food becomes more efficient and directed towards energizing exercise, rather than laying down fat. In addition the blood vessels are stimulated to keep open and free from fatty deposits.

When aerobic exercise is performed in conjunction with diet correction, the whole body benefits from the combined effects, and the bodyweight can effectively be controlled. This is a key issue for many athletes, whether it be in controlling the bodyweight within tight limits as is required in the majority of events, or ensuring that muscles are built, rather than fat deposited, in the heavy events.

Sleep Control

Many athletes suffer from sleep-control problems during both training periods and competition, and aerobic training is reported to have useful effects in this area. This is probably due to the general analgesic effect of natural endorphins produced as a result of such training, enabling the body to relax more easily after exercise. This also applies to other forms of extensive training. Clearly aerobic training is not a panacea in this respect, but it does make a contribution that many athletes find consistent and helpful during stressful times.

Improved Mental Focus

Improved focus is considered to be another of the effects of aerobic conditioning. The lower heart rate and the relaxation that are essential elements of such work enable athletes to learn the necessary skills to improve their concentration and mental focus during other unrelated activities, and in the competition scenario.

Fig 91. Low body fat of the trained athlete.

Improved Recovery from Exercise

Recovery is one of the most important aspects of athletes' training, and is often ignored in the ever more frenetic search for better performance. Recovery is the other side of the body's adaptation process, and, without sufficient recovery, the processes leading to improvement rapidly grind to a halt, and often end in breakdown.

Aerobic conditioning increases the speed of recovery by improving the body's transport systems via which the breakdown prod-ucts and unwanted metabolites are taken to the liver and kidneys for removal from the blood.

SUMMARY

Aerobic conditioning is an essential part of all athletes' training programmes, having many directly and indirectly beneficial effects. It is simple to perform and should be related to the necessary elements of the event for which the athlete is training. There are many variations of exercise type that produce very similar results, but there is much less crossover between sports and events than is generally supposed. Specificity then, should be an important aspect of the sessions.

A number of subsidiary effects of aerobic conditioning are beneficial to the athlete and also, of course, to the general public. Having said that, although this is generally true, there are, however, those in whom other serious deleterious problems override the helpful consequences of aerobic work.

CHAPTER 5
Anaerobic Conditioning

With the exception of the longer endurance events, there is a high element of anaerobic energy production and utilization in the majority of track and field events. There are two main processes related to the different cellular anaerobic energy production systems which are present in the two types of fast-contracting muscle fibres. These processes involve the formation of ATP by the production of lactic acid and by the breakdown of creatine phosphate.

The former is inefficient and the lactic acid accumulated eventually poisons the system, causing a dramatic decrease in the ability to perform muscular exercise. Anyone who has run a 400m flat out will understand the nature of this poisoning. The muscle fibres that primarily adopt this energy-production system are medium–fast contracting and used during extended sprints, in events from 200m to marathon. This type of anaerobic activity is called 'long-term'.

The breakdown of creatine to form ATP is very efficient, and is related to the contraction of very fast muscle fibres, the so-called fast-twitch fibres. These are responsible for the ability to run flat out for between 8 and 12sec, and thus are significant in all sprint events, but most effective in the distances up to 100m and the field events. This type of anaerobic activity is called 'short-term'.

It is therefore essential for all events to include some elements of anaerobic conditioning in the overall training programme. For 100m, anaerobic conditioning is a very high priority, as opposed to the marathon where it is a more subsidiary element. In general, anaerobic work is the essential conditioning element in most athletes' programmes.

One-off explosive muscle contraction is thought to have an additional element in the utilization of the very small quantities of ATP that exist in the muscle fibres at all times. It is also related to plyometric ability.

Fig 92. Middle-distance runners.

Both of these will be discussed at length in later chapters.

LONG-TERM ANAEROBIC CONDITIONING

All activities that are of sufficient intensity to cause the formation of lactic acid require long-term anaerobic conditioning. There is a wide variety of sessions that will help with this, and we will discuss several different types as examples of such training. There is circuit and lightweight and bodyweight stage training, discussed in later chapters; and speed endurance running, investigated below.

Speed Endurance Running

Speed endurance work is an essential technique for all runners – even the marathon runners require a sprint finish after all the aerobic work. It entails a session of fast runs completed in a series, with 'adequate' – not complete – recovery between repetitions. This means that each successive run is started *before* lactic acid is cleared from the system.

Defining adequate 'recovery', a process that has been well researched over the years, is essential on an individual basis. Simply speaking full recovery is the time taken for the pulse rate to return to normal after a period of exercise. Adequate recovery (also called 'worthwhile break') is defined as one third of the full recovery time. The graph below shows this relationship.

The actual figure needs to be assessed in the practical environment for each individual. Despite this appearing to be an arbitrary value, in practice the use of 'adequate recovery' sets a measurable parameter according to which training can be planned. The use of 'adequate recovery' is, of course, most significant to endurance athletes as part of their main training; however, it is also of significance to all events in the setting of basic

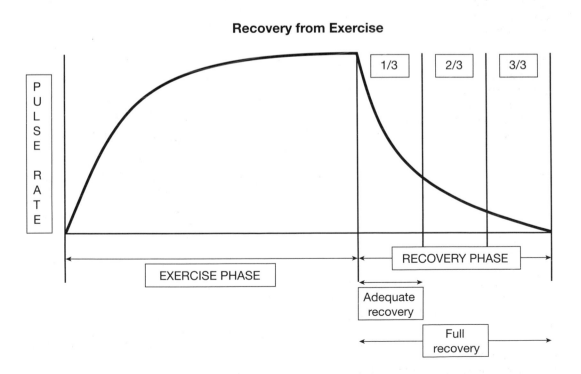

Recovery from Exercise

anaerobic conditioning levels, and as a test to look for improvement.

'Adequate recovery' is at the heart of speed endurance and other interval-type sessions, which are based on a burst of anaerobic (or aerobic) activity, followed by a rest, then a second burst of activity, and so on. Thus the athlete starts the second and subsequent exercise phases before complete recovery has occurred and the lactic acid completely removed from the body.

In the case of speed endurance, the exercise phases are fast sprints, the object being to try to sustain speed over the repetitions; as the session progresses this maintenance becomes more and more difficult. The body then adapts to the stress imposed and the athlete, over a period of time, becomes more able to sustain his or her speed under the duress of fatigue. Such training is very important for all running, jumping and throwing, although in the latter events only the javelin requires this to be a significant focal part of training.

The recent use of blood lactate analysis led to the introduction of the concept of 'lactate threshold', meaning the level of exercise at which the lactic acid in the blood starts to increase. There is a problem with this, however, since the lactate level does not suddenly rise, but increases according to a curve. It is usually accepted that the start of this curve is the threshold and, using this, very useful results have been obtained, particularly in cycling. The technique, however, should only be used at the top end of the sport, as it is complex and time-consuming.

Fartlek Training

This method is normally used by endurance athletes as an aerobic technique; however, by increasing the speed of the fast sections it can be modified to have a very effective role in anaerobic training. Essentially Fartlek involves running fast for a set distance or time, followed by jogging to recover. This cycle is repeated a number of times according to the need of the athlete. It is different from simple repetition speed running in that it is performed as a continuous run, normally over varying terrain. The adaptation that this encourages gives additional mental and physical strength to the athlete.

Specific Anaerobic Gymnasium Work

The gymnasium is not usually associated with endurance training, but, as we shall see, with bodyweight circuit and stage training, it can be a very effective addition to the methods of endurance coaches. Over and above these two methods is a more specific one that is very useful in rehabilitating injuries and improving specific muscular endurance weaknesses: this is the use of light weights performed with very high repetitions. For example, the simple squat works the leg muscles very effectively. If very light weights are used with high repetitions the exercise ceases to be strengthening and moves into the long-term anaerobic field. Because it is easily controllable, the coach can work the required muscles very hard and for whatever time-span is desired, under full control and immediate observation.

In addition, by varying the speed of repetition and the recovery, a similar lactate production can be produced to that experienced in an event. Using more event-specific exercises, and relating the performance of the exercise to the event – the frequency of repetition matching the running cadence, for example – further increases the usefulness of the method.

SHORT-TERM ANAEROBIC CONDITIONING

This can be split into two separate areas of focus: first, the anaerobic training needed for the sprinter (short-term anaerobic activities); and, second, the one-off maximum-effort training that is required for the sprint start and a jump or throw (explosive anaerobic activities). The former is based on the breakdown of creatine phosphate to produce the needed energy for muscle contraction, and the latter on the use of the minute residual stores of ATP combined with reactive strength and speed.

Fig 93. Sprint start.

Short-term Anaerobic Activities

Short-term anaerobic activities require very hard and specific conditioning methods to ensure improvement. These will include flat-out sprinting with full recovery, interval training at very fast speeds with adequate recovery, plyometrics and gymnasium work. In addition it would seem that nutrition can greatly influence the athlete's ability to perform at this speed, and recent research has suggested that many athletes are depleted in creatine either through poor diets or as a result of hard training. Replacement and supplementation are therefore the norm nowadays.

A word of caution, however: the ingestion of too much of this supplement can lead to serious cramping and muscle damage. The normal athlete's credo of 'more is better' must simply not be applied, and very careful experimentation must be used in assessing whether the athlete a) needs supplementation, or b) is overdosing. Any use of creatine should be very carefully monitored for results and potential reactions.

A combination of these four methods above, if applied appropriately, will improve the athlete's ability to sprint. The correct balance depends on the coach's plan for the year, but all elements are required to produce the best results. Most sprinters will do little flat-out sprinting except in competition, but they will do considerable fast interval training and plyometrics, as well as gym work. There is considerable variation in ideas on what balance to aim at, but the truth is really that every athlete is different and requires an individualized approach, except for the most basic of anaerobic conditioning.

Simple tests are needed to assess the athlete's state. These can include timed flat-out short runs or intervals, but the coach must know how the athlete responds to this type of test in order to interpret the results. A simple gymnasium test is also very useful to estimate short-term anaerobic fitness: this can be a test to measure the recovery of the heart rate after a series of activities designed to push up the production of lactic acid close to exhaustion. This can be achieved by performing a general exercise (for example, maximum number of squat thrusts performed in a minute) while recording the pulse rate. At the end of the exercise the rate should be pushing 200, and it should drop rapidly on cessation – a

Figs 94 & 95.
Squat thrust test.

guideline would be for it to return to below 100 in a minute.

Interestingly, this test can pick up certain problems that the athlete has, such as over-training and the onset of a cold or flu. In these circumstances the pulse simply stays high for much longer than normal.

Explosive Anaerobic Activities

Explosive ability seems to be closely related to the power and skill of the athlete, as well as to his or her metabolism. But even if the athlete performs a simple standing long jump, there is still a technical element that

Fig 96. Standing long jump.

needs to be taken into consideration, particularly for young and inexperienced athletes, if the test is to be a valid means of assessing this ability. However, this and the standing vertical jump are probably the best ways of testing leg explosive ability for a wide range of athletes.

Even so, each event might need a more specific test: for example, a discus thrower might want to test for arm explosive ability, and this might be assessed by isolating the throwing arm and testing its ability to throw a discus. Likewise a timed sprint start would help that athlete in estimating the

Fig 97. Maximum weight power clean.

explosive aspect of the initial phase of a sprint.

Conditioning to improve explosive anaerobic ability is a different problem, and little research has been performed on its general aspects and the efficacy of various training methods. The difficulty is in establishing whether or not an activity involves maximum explosive force generation or not: the difference between maximum and slightly sub-maximal is very small, and often athletes will perform within the 'comfort zone' and not work at absolute maximum output.

If we consider weight lifting, in which the lifter must perform the basic clean movement at peak effort, this might indicate a possible training method applicable to other sports. It has been generally accepted that such one-off efforts do have an improving effect on explosive ability, and it would seem reasonable that this could be utilized within the training regime of all explosive athletes to improve them, or at least condition them, ready for their event-specific work. There is no doubt that maximum weight power cleans can improve the ability to sprint start and throw, and the use of such work as a conditioning tool may be as close as we can get to the ultimate speed explosive effort with simple apparatus.

Since we are only looking for the single effort, there is no need to perform lots of repetitions; it is more significant to work on eight to ten single efforts with an increasing resistance. For weight lifters, the lowest weight considered appropriate for improvement is above 90 per cent of maximum. This produces a very hard session even if only one lift is used, but the results are usually good, and the difficulties of learning how to lift properly are small compared with possible benefits.

The throwers can use the power snatch as the basic exercise since this, although technically far more difficult than the clean, utilizes the arms and shoulders more, thus being more specific to the events.

SUMMARY

Anaerobic conditioning is a complex subject, and the various aspects relating to the energy-production pathways need to be understood sufficiently well for the coach to apply the derived principles effectively. For the long- and middle-distance runner, anaerobic conditioning needs to be focused largely on the long term, whereas the sprinters and throwers need to work at short-term and explosive aspects. The tolerance and clearance from the body of lactic acid is not very relevant to the faster events except during training, so no great emphasis needs to be applied in the training of athletes in those events.

The correct balance of anaerobic conditioning methods needs to be based on an accurate analysis of the needs of the event, as with all other conditioning activities. There is nothing worse for the athlete than to be told to work hard and painfully at something that is largely irrelevant to the event.

CHAPTER 6
Speed and Power

The basic speed of any athlete is determined by the proportion of fast-twitch muscles that his or her muscles contain. This proportion is largely genetic, but it can be influenced by the type of training that the athlete performs. These anaerobic muscle fibres are of two sorts, fast and faster, the former being largely fuelled by the breakdown of carbohydrate into lactic acid, and the latter by the breakdown of creatine phosphate to form creatine. In both, the important product from the muscle's point of view is adenosine tri-phosphate (ATP), which is the primary energy source for all muscular contraction: the faster that this is available, the faster the muscle can contract.

Flat-out speed of movement is produced by the fastest fibres contracting as fast, and in as great a number, as possible. Thus the shot-putter, for example, accelerates the implement to its maximal speed by finally flicking it off the finger tips, having accelerated it using the legs, body, back and arms prior to the release. This sequential development of speed is the hallmark of all athletic speed and therefore necessitates high neuro-muscular co-ordination as well as just basic speed of muscle contraction. Such rapid movements also require sufficient strength to move the resistance involved, be it the shot, or only the body, as in sprinting. The combination of speed and strength gives power, mathematically the product of speed multiplied by strength.

Interestingly, basic speed, it seems, can only be increased by around 10 per cent from its initial state, this improvement probably being related to better co-ordination within the neuro-muscular pathways. Strength, on the other hand, can be improved by up to 400 per cent above its initial level. On the face of it, this will mean that power, and therefore the ability to move fast, can be better increased by strength training than by speed training by a factor of forty. This is obviously very significant for athletes who need to adopt the most effective training regimens to produce near-potential performance.

This relationship is, of course, not that simple, because other factors such as bodyweight, range of movement and co-ordination are all changed when strength increases. The power may increase, but these other factors may have a negative effect on applying that power, so there is not a straight line relationship between strength increase and speed of movement, a fact that has often been ignored by coaches when strengthening athletes for an improvement in power and therefore speed.

POWER AND BODYWEIGHT

The downside of strength training is that the bodyweight tends to increase concomitantly with strength, because the muscle fibres grow bigger (hypertrophy) to produce greater force. For the shot-putter this is of little consequence within very broad limits, but for the sprinter or long jumper, any increase in bodyweight negatively affects his or her performance, as it is the body only that needs to be moved.

In the initial stages of strength training the muscles can actually shrink, because excess fat around the muscles and between bundles of fibres is removed. This also makes the contraction more efficient, since the pull of the muscles becomes nearer to a straight line. Accompanying this is increased vascularization, which has little effect on mass, but increases the size of the muscle when active. The net result is that the muscles become lighter and their definition becomes more refined. During this stage – whose duration varies, depending on the amount of strength training performed – there is a marked increase in power compared with the bodyweight, and thus usually a rapid increase in speed of movement.

As the effect of these preliminary factors dwindles, the only improvement comes from hypertrophy of the muscle, which is an actual increase in the size of the muscle fibres involved. This, then, causes an increase in muscular bulk and weight. At this point, great care must be taken in balancing strength increase with bodyweight increase: for most athletes it is useless simply increasing strength, but then negating its effect by an increase in bodyweight.

Power-for-weight Ratio

The power-for-weight ratio ([speed × strength]/bodyweight) is a somewhat simplistic but very useful measure of whether the athlete is making useful strength gains compared with his or her bodyweight. The comparison can be made by simply performing a standing long jump, a simple exercise technically, which measures how powerful the athlete is compared with the bodyweight.

If the standing long jump is measured over the training span of an athlete, initially it increases rapidly from around 1.5m for a beginner, up to 3m for men, and around 2.5m for women. From here on, progress is much harder, with the best recorded jumps being in the region of 3.8m for men, and 3m for women. It may take as long to improve from 3m to 3.5m as it did to go from 1.5m to 3m.

This is one reason why the emphasis of any strength training must change as the athlete progresses in his or her career. It is counter-productive to pile on the strength when little or no increase in power compared with bodyweight is being achieved. At this point, event technical factors become more significant, and thus strength training ceases to be a method for increasing power and tends to be used to enhance specific weaknesses within the technique.

Many athletes simply maintain their strength and power in the latter stages of their careers, concentrating rather on refining their techniques.

PLYOMETRIC TRAINING

A considerable amount of research has been done into methods for increasing athletic power, but, over and above basic strength training, there has been little methodology developed that has proved effective. The most significant technique suggested over the last thirty years is that of plyometrics, the training of the reactive ability of muscles. This conditioning technique consists of repeated reactive movements such as bounding, hopping and jumping. For certain athletic events – particularly the sprints and jumps – plyometrics is a valuable and effective method for increasing power. It takes considerable work to enhance the reactive abilities, and such training is very stressful on the joints, ligaments and tendons, often leading to injury if the sessions are not very carefully controlled.

The object of plyometrics is to enhance the athlete's ability to react after landing one or two feet on the ground. This reactive ability is based on the stretch–recoil function of the tendons, the muscular stretch reflexes, and the conscious muscle contractions, all of which make up an athlete's response to landing on the ground. Because the nature of such reactions is one of attempting to respond with maximum speed, they are by definition very vigorous to perform, but potentially effective in producing an increase in speed of movement.

Some athletic events, such as the jumps, require high levels of plyometric ability in the legs, others do not. The long jumper needs the most rapid reaction in the ankle at take-off, whereas the discus thrower requires that the rear foot pivots on the ground when it

Fig 98. Bounding.

lands after the turn, rather than reactively lifting off. For the discus thrower there is a plyometric requirement in the chest and shoulder at delivery, and plyometric training of these muscles can be an effective training method for the event.

It is therefore very important for the coach not to accept blindly that all plyometrics will help their event, but to analyse the way the muscles and tendons operate in each segment of the body used.

Hopping, Bounding and Jumping

One problem with plyometric activities is that the best reaction is gained from a very hard surface – but anyone who has tried to jump on concrete will know that it is also very punishing. Using the modern track surface is somewhat easier on the joints, but even this has problems, as the track surface tends to create a reaction itself to the force applied by the athlete and so there is a second uncontrollable force being applied as the athlete hops, bounds or jumps. For the untrained this can lead to 'shin-splints' (damage to the attachment of the *tibialis anterior* muscle to the shin bone), or even damage to the tibia itself.

It is therefore essential to condition the young or inexperienced athlete slowly and very carefully before the most vigorous plyometric activities are adopted as part of the training regime. Any simple activity, such as repetition two-footed jumping and hopping through sand, is a useful starting point, as many young athletes are not strong enough to take the force of landing from even a minimal height, and the sand provides a safe and soft surface if the stresses are too great. Progression can be slow and controlled, and the athlete will gain confidence in his or her abilities and skills to perform the activities correctly. This process should last a full winter's training. After this, training can move forwards and gentle jumping, hopping and bounding on an all-weather track surface can be started safely, though if there are any signs of shin soreness the activity must be halted immediately and a further period of sand conditioning instigated.

The rule of thumb for plyometrics is that the reaction *must* be as fast as possible and as near to maximum speed as possible. The exercises cease to be plyometric if there is a pause or noticeable slowing of the reaction because the force is too great to overcome.

Hurdle Jumping

Hurdle jumping is the single most dangerous activity in the list of conditioning methods. It involves the athlete jumping two-footed over a series of hurdles of a set height. It is strongly recommended that any form of hurdle jumping is not used at an early stage in progress, because it forces the athlete into potentially uncontrollable landing positions, and thus ceases to be plyometric. It is far better to make the athletes perform unrestricted jumps, as this will allow for the variation in ability that there will inevitably be among a group of developing athletes, and ensure that each individual reacts as near to maximum speed as possible.

Even so, hurdle jumping is one of the most frequently used training methods, and, often, little thought is given to why the coach should expose the athletes to such a potentially disastrous method. It is vital that only the most able and well-conditioned athletes perform this activity, and only then if there are no signs of injury arising from its use.

Fig 99. Sand jumping.

Figs 100, 101 & 102.
Hurdle jumping.

Fig 103. Step jumping.

Box or Step Jumping

Box or step jumping involves the athlete jumping up on to, and/or off, solid boxes. It is a more controllable exercise than hurdle jumping, but can still be potentially dangerous for the unskilled and unconditioned athlete. However, if used sensibly and progressively, box jumping is a most effective and efficient method for increasing reactive strength and therefore power.

It is suggested that all athletes start with very low boxes, perhaps of no more than 30cm in height. Plyometric conditioning at such a low level allows the athlete to experience the forces without exposing them to anything more than light stress. The better athletes will jump higher on to and off the boxes, while the less able will be able to manage some form of reactive jumps.

Progression is managed by increasing the height of the boxes or the number of jumps performed, both of which will have beneficial effects on the reactive abilities of the athlete. But care must be taken, as with all plyometric conditioning methods, to ensure that the athletes are coping and that no injuries are starting to develop.

In the early years of using box jumping, it was popular for coaches to boast about the height from which their athletes could jump and still react. This, however, proved to be counterproductive, since in many cases severe injuries were sustained (as with hurdle jumping). The rule of thumb should be that the athlete can react strongly from whatever height box is used. This, after all, is the purpose of the activity – it is not to see who can remain in one piece.

Chest and Shoulder Plyometrics

This type of exercise is not often seen in training schedules, yet it has a very important part to play in the shot put, and discus and javelin throws. Because the muscles involved are weaker than the legs, much care must be taken not to overstress them. The best example of a chest and shoulder plyometric is the discus arm/shoulder exercise used by the German athletes to help their discus throwers. This is simply performed by the athlete lying on his or her back horizontally along a high box with the shoulders and head over the end and the feet held in position. The throwing arm is then extended at right angles to the body, and the arm dropped towards the ground. When at its full-range position a medicine ball is dropped on to the hand, and the athlete must then react by throwing it up vertically.

Clearly, care must be taken in selecting the weight of the ball and deciding on what height to drop it from. A guideline is to use a small 2–5kg ball initially, dropped from no more than 30cm above the hand. Practice will determine the exact weight and height for each athlete, but the important thing to remember is that the reaction must be fast, not laboured and slow.

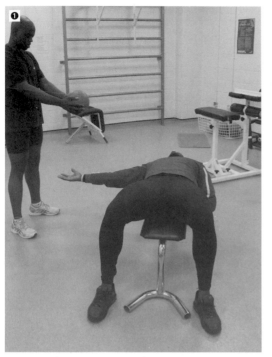

Figs 104, 105, 106 & 107.
Discus arm/shoulder plyometric exercise.

FAST WEIGHT TRAINING

Weight training can be a most effective way of increasing power, since it is the most direct way of increasing strength. Chapter 10 deals with basic strength training, so here we will limit ourselves to looking at weight training for power.

Generally speaking, the most often used power weight exercises are the power clean and power snatch; others include squat jumps, step-ups and jumping/hopping with a bar-bell. These are all good exercises if performed in the proper way, which is for maximum range and maximum speed. Sometimes coaches become involved in the intricate *techniques* of weight lifting: these, however, are designed only to make the athlete lift the maximum weight, which in fact has little relevance to most athletes as their require-ments are for strength and thus power over the maximum range, not the maximum weight lifted over the shortest range. Such exercises as squat clean or snatch are there-fore not part of an athlete's programme, except perhaps for the heavy athletes who might use them as a diversion from their real work.

There has been ongoing discussion about what resistance will produce maximum power increases, and there are several schools of thought relating to the best and quickest way to increase power using weight training. The truth seems to be that most methods have some effect as long as the movements are simple and fast, and the resistance suffi-cient. This is useful, as it provides the coach with a variety of ways to do the same job, and he or she can therefore keep the train-ing interesting.

Fig 108. Power bench press.

Medium-resistance, Low-repetition Weight Training

There is one school of thought that suggests that maximum power output and therefore best training effect is produced at between 40 and 45 per cent of best single repetition performance. There is no doubt that there does seem to be an increase in power if this level of training is used when the movement is at maximum speed. For most athletes only three repetitions can be performed at maximum power, and the proponents of the method suggest that no further repetitions should be performed if the power output drops. This type of training therefore requires many sets of low repetitions (for example, ten sets of three repetitions), which tends to be mentally boring and difficult to assess in terms of results. It is nevertheless effective as a method for short periods of the year when an uplift in mental and physical power is needed.

The three basic exercises most often used are bench press, power snatch and squat, but there is no reason to restrict the session to these, since with a little thought more specific exercises can be introduced, for example by using single-sided dumb-bell work such as the shot press, or single-arm snatch.

Light-resistance, Medium-repetition Weight Training

Light-resistance (20–30 per cent of single repetition maximum) weight training is probably the most difficult of such work to perform. It is very easy for the athlete to achieve inconsistent output because, as fatigue sets in, often the level of work drops more as a result of mental weariness than actual physical difficulty. It is therefore vital that, if such sessions are to be included in the programme, they are used sparingly, and only when the athlete is intent on maximum effort. Results will simply not come if the exercises are performed at less than maximum speed.

Having tried many variations on this theme, the only one that has proved consistently effective is the 'Winch Power Session'. It is based on work reported from East European coaches when under Communist rule in the early 1980s, and consists of a series of exercises performed with a resistance that allows five repetitions to be managed in 6sec; anything slower, and its effectiveness decreases. A rest of 10sec is then allowed between each of four sets of the exercises, and 15sec between exercises. For example:

– 4 sets of 5 power cleans at 15% of single maximum resistance with 10sec recovery
15sec rest

– 4 sets of 5 inclined sit-ups at 30 degrees incline with 10sec recovery
15sec rest

– 4 sets of 5 bent-over rowing at 20% of single maximum resistance with 10sec recovery
15sec rest

– 4 sets of 5 bench presses at 20% of single maximum resistance with 10sec recovery
15sec rest

– 4 sets of 5 squats at 20% of single maximum resistance with 10sec recovery
15sec rest

– 4 sets of 5 power snatches at 15% of single maximum resistance with 10sec recovery

When performed once a week for four to six weeks, this session seems to produce a marked increase in power, as measured by the standing long jump. I have found it is the only session that will do this in the short training time involved, and for this reason it is, in my opinion, an excellent session for peak or pre-peak training.

SUMMARY

Speed is the most important element of every event, even the marathon: the fastest athlete normally wins, assuming technique is good. Power is the result of applying force quickly, and the greater the force the higher the power, assuming speed is maintained. This gives a guide as to how power can be developed, namely by the use of strength training and the maintenance of speed.

Conditioning for speed and power requires the athlete to operate at all times with maximum speed, even when lifting heavy weights; in this way his or her speed will stay as high as possible as strength increases. A number of advanced techniques assist in combining strength and speed with a resultant increase in power. These are difficult to perform as they require total commitment in order to operate at the highest possible speed while performing fairly complex movements.

The eventual power output is dependent on the co-ordination of raw power with the highly technical movements involved in most athletic events, and to maximize this requires time, skill and patience.

CHAPTER 7
Circuit Training

Circuit training is one of the most commonly used exercise systems in athletics. Virtually every athlete, young and older, has experienced the fun and pain of this system as part of their build-up to becoming a star. The effects are mainly aerobic and general anaerobic and, depending on the emphasis, can be used to help local muscular endurance. The best aspect of circuits is that they are infinitely variable and can thus maintain the athletes' interest and application over a long period while having the same or a similar physiological effect.

The key to successful circuit training is the accuracy of the performance of each exercise. So often athletes will sacrifice technique for speed, but the coach must never allow this – and once they know that the coach will not tolerate any variation from strict technique, they will accept it as the norm and so perform to a higher standard.

The basic system entails doing a single set of a series of carefully structured exercises with no rest between sets. This cycle is then repeated, again with no rest between cycles, a number of times, usually between three and six. Each exercise is normally performed either for a defined number of repetitions or for a specified period of time. Some examples are shown below.

Improvement is attempted by either increasing the repetitions or times for each exercise, by increasing the number of circuits, or by speeding up the whole session. Normally the circuit would be repeated three, then four, five and six times in consecutive weeks, and, when six circuits have been reached, the time for the overall session should be decreased, though without sacrificing technique.

The number of repetitions or the time loading can be changed for a specific athlete or a specific purpose. For example, should the coach wish to work on the body core, then the emphasis would reflect that by including extra mid-region exercises, or more

Repetition-based:	Exercise 1	10 repetitions	General – all body
	Exercise 2	10 repetitions	Leg jumping
	Exercise 3	10 repetitions	Abdominal
	Exercise 4	10 repetitions	Lower back/hamstrings
	Exercise 5	10 repetitions	Abdominal
	Exercise 6	10 repetitions	Lower back/hamstrings
	Exercise 7	10 repetitions	Arms push
	Exercise 8	15 repetitions	Calves
Time-based:	Exercise 1	30 seconds	General – all body
	Exercise 2	20 seconds	Leg jumping
	Exercise 3	30 seconds	Abdominal
	Exercise 4	30 seconds	Lower back/hamstrings
	Exercise 5	20 seconds	Abdominal
	Exercise 6	30 seconds	Lower back/hamstrings
	Exercise 7	20 seconds	Arms push
	Exercise 8	30 seconds	Calves

repetitions on those exercises, or more time on each; the same would apply for the legs, and so on. Thus we have a very variable session base that can be tailored to training, or to individual needs and focus. In addition, the balance between aerobic and anaerobic can be adjusted, depending on the work rate and the resulting pulse rate during the session. Working within the aerobic range will make the session more aerobic, and working within the anaerobic range will orientate it towards the anaerobic.

Combined with simple and effective tests, the circuit can help the athlete maintain a balance of fitness and local muscular endurance throughout the year.

SAMPLE SESSIONS

All these exercises can be used in the body-weight stage training sessions described in the next chapter, as well as in circuits.

Session 1

Burpees
Suggested initial repetitions/time:
10 repetitions / 20 seconds

Figs 109, 110, 111, 112 & 113. Burpees.

This is a time-honoured exercise that most athletes find very tiring. Its advantage, however, is that it works the whole body, and is therefore an excellent starting point for a circuit. It is basically a squat thrust followed by a star jump. The squat thrust element is performed by starting in a press-up position with the body stretched out horizontally; from here the legs are brought forwards, the knees finishing just inside the elbows (not outside). The star jump is then completed with arms and head reaching tall. On landing, the body is returned to the knees-forward position, and then to the starting position. It is important to develop a rhythm and to make sure that all positions are fully extended. Speed tends to shorten the move-ments, making them less effective in stimu-lating the whole body.

Calf jumps
Suggested initial repetitions/time:
15 repetitions / 20 seconds

This is an excellent exercise for reactive calf training. It is performed by hardly bending the legs, and creating a jumping action with the calves only. The movement should be bouncy, and a clear effort made to involve the quads as little as possible. The athlete should also try to pick the toes up in each repetition so that the foot moves into the neutral posi-tion in the middle of each repetition. This neutral foot position is where the foot is near

Figs 114 & 115. Calf jumps.

to 90 degrees flexed and relaxed; the bounce following will then involve all the necessary elements to work the calves and Achilles tendons. If there is tightness on landing each repetition the jerkiness of the subsequent bounces can be injurious, and is certainly less effective in developing reactive conditioning.

Alternate-leg 'V' sits
Suggested initial repetitions/time:
8 × left + 8 × right / 20 seconds

Alternate-leg 'V' sits are performed by lying flat on the floor, arms and legs extended and touching the ground. From here, one leg is raised and the body curled up so that the hands reach for, and touch, the toes of the raised foot. The starting position is then resumed, and the other leg raised and the toes touched. This is repeated smoothly so that a rhythm is set up. It is vital that the toes are touched and not the ankle, as the latter effectively shortens the movement and reduces its effectiveness.

Flat twisting-back hyperextensions
(2sec hold in final position)
Suggested initial repetitions/time:
6 × left + 6 × right / 30 seconds

This exercise works the lower back in a rotational fashion and is performed by lying on the front with the hands held behind the

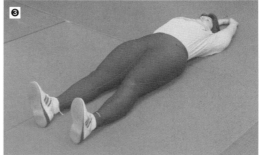

Figs 116, 117, 118 & 119. Alternate-leg 'V' sits.

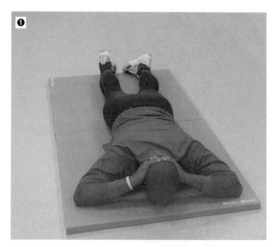

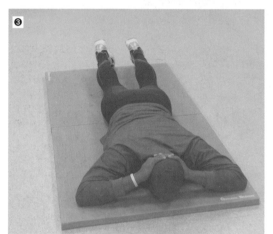

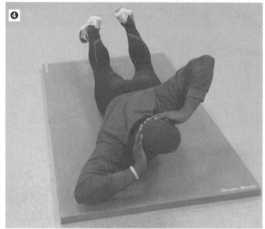

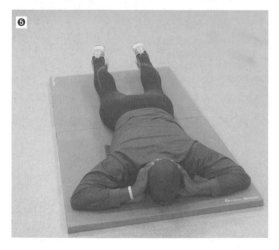

Figs 120, 121, 122, 123 & 124. Flat twisting-back hyperextensions.

Figs 125 & 126.
Feet flat crunches.

ears. From here, the back is arched back and one shoulder twisted to the side and held in that position for 2sec. The start position is resumed, and the next repetition is initiated with a twist to the other side. The movement should be performed smoothly: any jerking into position may cause cramping.

Feet flat crunches
(2sec hold in final position)
Suggested initial repetitions/time:
10 repetitions / 30 seconds

This is one of the simplest and most effective abdominal exercises. The athlete lies on his or her back with the knees bent to 90

Figs 127 & 128. Feet raised sit-ups.

Figs 129, 130 & 131. Low box jumps.

degrees and the arms crossed in front of the chest or held with the hands lightly resting against the head, just behind the ears. The stomach is flattened and the shoulders lifted towards the knees without taking the lower back off the ground so that the stomach is 'crunched' between chest and knees. This position is held for 2sec, and the starting position is then resumed. The key factor in this exercise is to keep the lower back firmly forced against the ground and not lifted off it.

Feet raised press-ups
(Feet raised on bench)
Suggested initial repetitions/time:
10 repetitions/ 30 seconds

Feet raised press-ups is a variation on the normal exercise. The feet are raised on to a bench or chair, and the normal press-up starting position assumed. From here the movement is performed as usual, the only difference being that it works the anterior deltoids and pectorals at a slightly different angle from normal. It is slightly harder to

perform, so if the athlete struggles, use only half range, or reduced repetitions or time.

Low box jumps
(About 30cm in height)
Suggested initial repetitions/time:
12 repetitions / 20 seconds

This is a useful exercise that works the reactive aspects of the leg. It is essentially a plyometric activity if performed correctly, but tends to become less so as the athlete tires. It is performed by jumping two-footed off a low box (with a maximum height of 30cm), and trying to jump in the air immediately on landing. Minimum leg bend should be used to focus on the calf/Achilles units, and the feet should be in the neutral position on landing. Care must be taken not to rush the movements, and to do them with particular care, as performing such reactive tasks well when tired needs consummate skill. As with all plyometric activities, this exercise is not advised for unconditioned novices.

Figs 132, 133, 134, 135, 136 & 137. Standing full-range body circles.

Figs 138, 139 & 140. Full narrow-stance split squat jumps.

Standing full-range body circles
Suggested initial repetitions/time:
6 × left + 6 × right / 20 seconds

Standing full-range body circling is not normally used in circuits, even though it is an excellent exercise for conditioning the mid-region muscles. It is performed by standing with the feet well astride. The arms are extended and then swept round in a circle touching the ground in the forward low position and up as far as possible in the upright position. The movement should be as extensively rangy and loose as possible, and smoothly performed. All the repetitions are completed in one direction, and then all in the other.

Session 2

Full narrow-stance split squat jumps
Suggested initial repetitions/time:
8 × left + 8 × right / 20 seconds

This is a variation on standard squat jumps, in which the feet are placed one back and one forward at the start of the exercise, but only narrowly apart. The athlete then bends fully, and jumps, and while in mid-air the feet are exchanged so that they are split the opposite way on landing. This is an excellent exercise for all athletic events because it uses the more natural one-foot-forward and one-foot-back position, thus relating more closely to the activities. In working each leg independently there are significant balance and posture elements that do not occur in the normal squat jump.

Alternate reverse leg raises
(2sec hold at final position)
Suggested initial repetitions/time:
8 × left + 8 × right / 30 seconds

This is an excellent exercise for the lower back, gluteals and hamstrings. It is performed by lying on the front with the arms outstretched and the hands grasping a firm

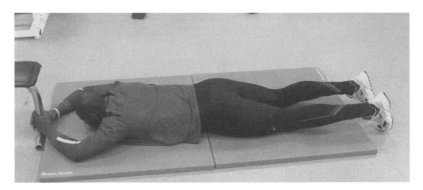

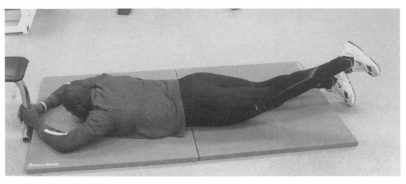

Figs 141, 142, 143, 144 & 145. Alternate reverse leg raises.

object such as a bench for stability. From here, one leg is raised and held for 2sec at the top position. The range is limited, but this is as it should be. It is very important not to rotate, and this can be avoided by keeping the hips flat on the ground. The movement is then repeated with the other leg.

Free sit-ups
(Hands behind head)
Suggested initial repetitions/time:
10 repetitions / 20 seconds

Free sit-ups form the basic exercise for the *rectus abdominis* muscles, and are performed by lying on the floor with the knees bent to 90 degrees. The hands are held behind the ears and are not allowed either to pull on the neck or move from the ears during the movement. The actual exercise is to curl the body up so that the chest approaches the knees, and then to sit back to the starting position with back flat. A conscious effort must be made to keep the lower back flat against the ground in the initial position so

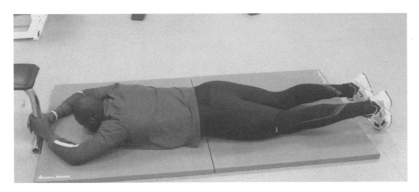

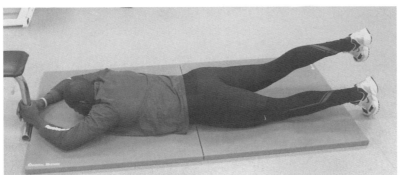

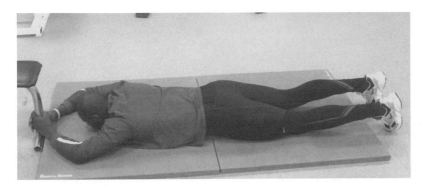

that no hyperextension occurs during the first part of the movement. Some athletes find this hard if they have poor core strength, and in this instance a sit-back rather than a sit-up is best: in the sit-back the athlete starts in the sitting-up position, and then curls backwards to the point where the lower back touches the ground, and no further. This is followed by sitting up to the starting position. The sit-back is excellent for remedial work in athletes who have lower back problems as it is easily controlled and does not involve any potential for hyperextension.

Figs 146 & 147. Free sit-ups.

Kneeling rotating lean-backs
Suggested initial repetitions/time:
8 × left + 8 × right / 20 seconds

This exercise is another for the mid-region, but this time for the rotational muscles. The athlete kneels on the ground with the feet flat and pointing back. Allowing the hips to sit back, one hand is taken round and placed to the back of, and between, the feet; the other arm is held across the chest at shoulder height. From here the back elbow is bent, thus forcing a rotation of the body, while at the same time reaching round to the rear with the loose arm. Once full range has been achieved, the movement is repeated in the opposite direction. It is important to ensure complete range is achieved and that the exercise does not degenerate into a loose rotating exercise with little stress involved: when performed properly the rotating muscles will feel as though they have been worked very hard.

Lunges with full body lean
Suggested initial repetitions/time:
8 × left + 8 × right / 20 seconds

Lunges are often used in circuits, but seldom performed in a strict manner. There are many variations, of which this is one. It is performed from a standing starting position with the feet together and the hands clasped behind the neck or with a light bar on the shoulders. From here, a long step forwards is taken on to a flat front foot, and the body bent forwards until the chest lies along the front thigh, with the eyes looking forwards. The front leg is then extended and the back straightened to return to the starting position. The lunge is then repeated with the other leg. The movement should be performed smoothly and accurately and care taken to keep it stable.

Step-up sprint drives
Suggested initial repetitions/time:
10 × left + 10 × right / 30 seconds

Step-ups are another of those exercises used in circuits without proper definition or

Figs 148, 149, 150, 151 & 152. Kneeling rotating lean-backs.

Figs 153 & 154. Lunges with full body lean.

control of movement. Generally speaking, correctly performed step-ups are a good exercise, but it is so easy to cheat on them that their use can become fairly meaningless. This version tends to prevent the athlete from rendering it useless, because once he or she has stepped on to the bench (which should be about 40cm in height), the trailing leg is driven upwards in a movement similar to that in the sprint start or long-jump take-off. The final position should be well balanced on the toes, with the arms working as in the sprint, before returning to the start where a pause

Figs 155 & 156.
Step-up sprint drives.

of 1sec should be implemented to prevent rebounding into the next repetition. The movement should be performed dynamically for the best results and range.

Feet raised bench dips
Suggested initial repetitions/time:
10 repetitions / 20 seconds

This form of bench dips, with the feet raised in front to the same height as the hands, is more difficult than the version where the feet rest on the ground. This is because, with the feet raised, more of the force is taken on the arms, and thus a greater resistance to straightening the arms after flexion is encountered. It also has the advantage of stretching the shoulder joint more and thus working the arm and shoulder pushing muscles over a greater range. It is not, however, an exercise for the unconditioned or weak, who should use the feet-on-floor version. Care should be taken to bend the arms as far as possible, allowing the buttocks to touch the ground if possible. The arms should then be completely straightened to complete the maximum range of movement for the exercise.

Sprint thrusts
Suggested initial repetitions/time:
12 × left + 12 × right / 20 seconds

Sprint thrusts are a seemingly easy version of squat thrusts, except that only one foot is brought forward at a time, with the knee tucking inside the arms, while the other foot is reached back as far as possible to create a wide split. In addition the hips are pushed upwards as the feet change position, to create a bouncy up-and-down movement rather than a backward-and-forward glide, as in the squat thrust. The exercise is not hard, but it does help in both getting used to splitting widely, and also in reacting from that position, a movement similar to that used in many athletic events. As with the other exercises, range should not be sacrificed for speed.

Session 3

Full wide-stance, split squat jumps
Suggested initial repetitions/time:
10 × left + 10 × right / 30 seconds

These are similar to the narrow-stance version described above, except that the split is wider and therefore more difficult to drive up from. Because of this the feet are not changed over during the jump. This makes the maintenance of control easier. The advantage of this exercise is that it stresses the gluteals and hamstrings significantly, working them over a large range of their action. It is most important in this exercise not just to swap the feet without the upward drive, which is the heart of the movement.

Alternate leg raise from hip raise
Suggested initial repetitions/time:
8 × left + 8 × right / 20 seconds

This is a difficult exercise, and should only be included for those who are well conditioned. It is performed by raising the hips into the basic hip raise position (the legs may be bent to make the position sustainable), supported on shoulders and heels, and alternately raising a single leg (with the leg straightening) to the horizontal. To execute this requires good core stability, but it also aids the further development of that stability. It must be performed carefully and steadily, avoiding jerky and unstable movements that might destabilize the basic position.

Double reverse leg raise
(2sec hold)
Suggested initial repetitions/time:
10 repetitions / 30 seconds

The double reverse leg raise is a powerful exercise for developing the lower back, gluteal and hamstring condition. To perform it correctly, the athlete lies flat on the ground face down, and holds on to a firm structure to the front of the head. This prevents the shoulders from lifting as the legs are raised

Figs 157, 158 & 159.
Feet raised bench dips.

Figs 160, 161, 162, 163 & 164.
Sprint thrusts.

Figs 165, 166, 167 & 168. Full wide-stance split squat jumps.

off the ground and held for 2sec at their high point. The legs should be straight when raised, for best effect. The legs are then lowered to the starting position, and the movement repeated.

'V' sits

Suggested initial repetitions/time:
10 repetitions / 20 seconds

'V' sits require co-ordination to perform, but this improves with repetition. The athlete lies flat on the floor, back down. The legs and arms are outstretched touching the ground, and, from here, both hands are raised and at the same time the legs are lifted. The object is to touch both hands on both feet by raising both arms and legs simultaneously into a 'V' position, and then returning to the starting point. It is important that each repetition is fully completed; if it is not, the full effect of the exercise is dramatically reduced.

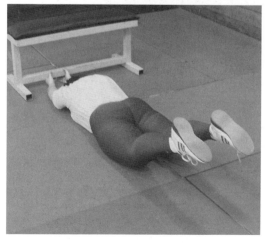

Figs 169 & 170. Alternate leg raise from hip raise. Figs 171 & 172. Double reverse leg raise.

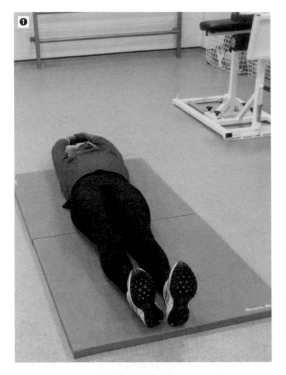

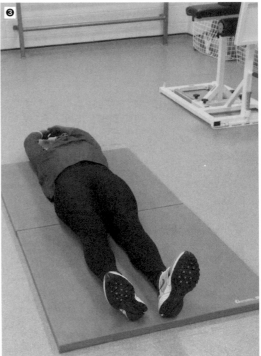

Figs 173, 174 & 175. 'V' sits.

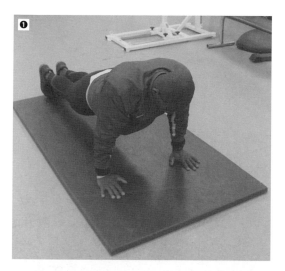

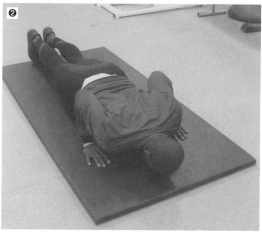

Figs 176, 177 & 178. Elbows tucked-in press-ups.

Elbows tucked-in press-ups
Suggested initial repetitions/time:
10 repetitions / 20 seconds

This form of press-up involves tucking the elbows into the sides, which in turn forces the hands to point forwards. This moves the emphasis of the exercise to the anterior deltoids and triceps muscles, and away from the pectorals. It is also more difficult to perform, but not dramatically so. An important feature of press-ups is that they aid core stability when performed well. This is because the body is held in a static linear position which necessitates the core stabilizers to be active throughout the exercise.

Step-up drives
Suggested initial repetitions/time:
8 × left + 8 × right / 30 seconds

Step-up drives allow the use of the step-up movement with a light to medium weight, but extending the movement by driving the knee up to the final position as in a long-jump take-off. The athlete starts by placing

Figs 179 & 180. Step-up drives.

the driving leg on to the bench, then pushing hard upwards, and pulling the trailing leg through and driving it up in front of the body. Care must be taken not to overdo the knee lift, as this can cause the athlete to become unstable and fall backwards. Again, this is a good all-round exercise that helps develop posture and stability during athletic movements, particularly in sprints and jumps.

Supported bounce jumps
Suggested initial repetitions/time:
15 repetitions / 20 seconds

This is a simple, safe and effective plyometric exercise. It is performed by standing upright close to some wall bars or other supporting structure such as a dipping bar. The hands are lightly placed on the support, and, after a shallow leg dip, the athlete jumps as high as possible, with additional upward push being supplied by the arms; this lifts him higher than by using just the legs alone, and

therefore creates a more forceful drop to the ground. The object is then to bounce immediately on landing and again to jump as high as possible. The emphasis is thus on jumping high and reacting on hitting the ground, the whole action being moderated by the supporting arm action. Care, however, must be taken not to use the arms except for support and slight lift at the end of the leg drive.

Lying abductor raises
(2sec hold in final position)
Suggested initial repetitions/time:
10 × left + 10 × right / 30 seconds

The abductor muscles are often neglected in conditioning programmes, except in events that specifically use them, such as the javelin throw. This exercise is simple and effective, but must be performed accurately to be of any use. The athlete lies on his or her side with the body and legs in a straight line. The head is rested on the hand, and the free arm

Figs 181, 182, 183 & 184. Supported bounce jumps.

is used to stabilize the position by resting on the ground. The foot of the upper leg is pulled into the neutral position (foot 90 degrees to shin), and then lifted to maximum position without any rotation: this latter is most important because rotation changes the movement from an abductor to a gluteal exercise. The leg is held in the top position for 2sec, and then lowered to the starting position and the action repeated.

SUMMARY

The sessions above are only examples of those that can be constructed. It is important, however, to make sure that in developing circuits you adhere to the general principles described in the first part of this chapter. The most important of these is to ensure that the whole body is exercised, and that any specific requirements are included as additional exercises. Never bias the session too far to one particular muscle group, because in the long run this can produce muscular imbalances. The accurate performance of each exercise is also vital, and skill should never be sacrificed for speed. The purpose of performing the circuit is to exercise different muscle groups properly, not to beat a world record.

Circuits should be designed to help the athletes, and should therefore contain appropriate exercises and be at an appropriate level of difficulty. Never set sessions to impress the athletes with how easy it is to cause pain; rather, always make the work enjoyable but hard.

OPPOSITE: Figs 185 & 186. Lying abductor raises.

CHAPTER 8
Bodyweight Stage Training

Stage training is a basic pattern of exercising that entails performing several sets of a single exercise, followed by several sets of another exercise, and then another, and so on, as in weight training. When using just bodyweight as resistance, this becomes bodyweight stage training and is an excellent form of local anaerobic work (local muscular endurance): by this it is meant that by doing three or four sets of an exercise, for example on the triceps, this specific muscle is working anaerobically.

Bodyweight stage training also has an aerobic element if the work is sustained with little or no recovery, and it also creates a small strengthening effect. This method of training is ideal for most athletes, and can be designed to improve specifically weak areas of the body.

Described below is an example of a simple session focused on the mid-region. All the exercises described can also be used in circuit training. It is, of course, possible to add in light resistance exercises such as dumb-bell sprint arm action or squat jumps with a light weight. The sessions are still defined as bodyweight, since the majority of the resistances are provided by the body alone.

The session following is specifically designed to aid endurance runners and jumpers.

GENERAL BODYWEIGHT STAGE TRAINING SESSION

Sample Session Structure

Squat Thrusts

This is a time-honoured exercise which, when performed properly, is most effective in working the whole body, and more specifically the hip flexors and *rectus abdominis* muscles.

To execute the correct movement the body starts in a strict press-up position, the body being held in line with the legs (without sagging of the hips). From here the legs are flexed, and the knees brought towards the arms and tucked just inside the elbows. In reaching this final position the feet are lifted off the ground and only touch down again at completion. The return to the starting position is achieved by reversing this movement. It is vital that the whole move-

Suggested initial sets and repetitions:

1]	Squat thrusts	4 × 10
2]	Press-ups	4 × 10
3]	Hip raises	4 × 10 (3sec hold at top)
4]	Free twisting sit-ups	4 × 6 left / 6 right alternately
5]	Flat back hyperextensions	4 × 10 (3sec hold at top)
6]	Chinnies	4 × 10 left / 10 right alternately
7]	Bench dips	4 × 10
8]	Full-range squat jumps	4 × 10

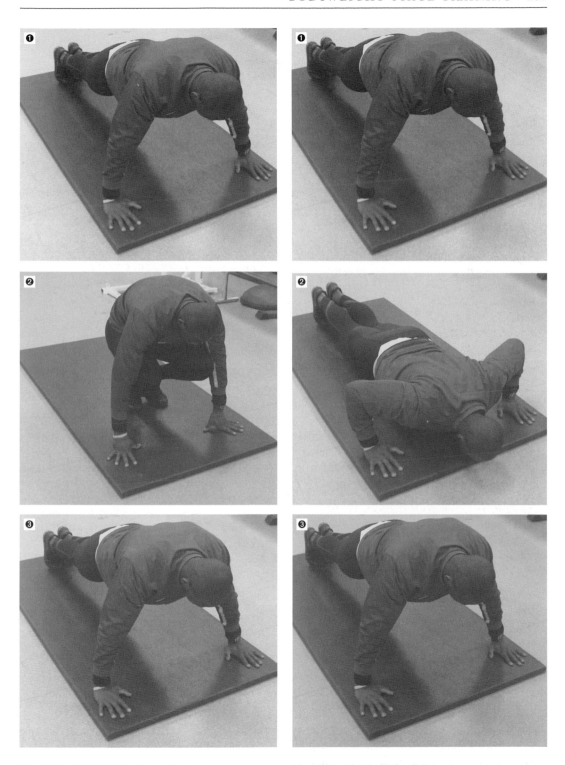

Figs 187, 188 & 189. Squat thrusts.　　　　Figs 190, 191 & 192. Press-ups.

ment is complete and correctly performed to obtain the best effect.

Press-ups

This is another 'standard', having been used for as long as anyone can remember; it works the triceps, anterior deltoids, pectorals and abdominal muscles.

It is performed by lying on the ground with the body extended and the feet together. The hands are normally placed slightly wider than the shoulders, with the elbows pointing to the rear. From here, the body is held rigid, and pushed up to arms' length in a controlled manner; it is then lowered steadily back to the ground. The exercise is ineffective if the body is allowed to sag or the backside to rise above the line of the rest of the body. At starting point the hips and chest must be touching the ground.

Variations on press-ups include the wide hand position that exercises the pectorals more, and the narrow hand position that exercises the triceps. For beginners, the exercise can be performed with the knees acting as the fulcrum, although the body must again be held straight from knee to shoulder.

A more advanced version is to have the feet raised on a bench or chair. This puts more of the bodyweight on to the arms, and is thus more difficult to perform. Another variation that is used by the throwers involves the press-up being followed by a further push on to the fingertips. This helps develop the wrist strength needed in the events.

There is also the one-armed version performed with the legs splayed wide, the non-active arm held behind the back, and the pushing arm tucked into the side of the body. This should only be used by advanced athletes, and only as a bit of fun as a variation.

Hip Raises

(3sec hold)
This is a simple but effective exercise that works the lower back and the other stabilizing core stability muscles of the mid-region.

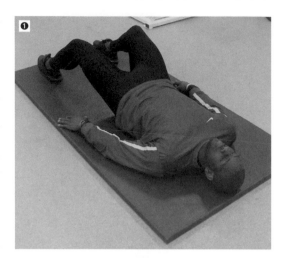

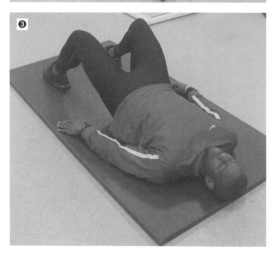

Figs 193, 194 & 195. Hip raises.

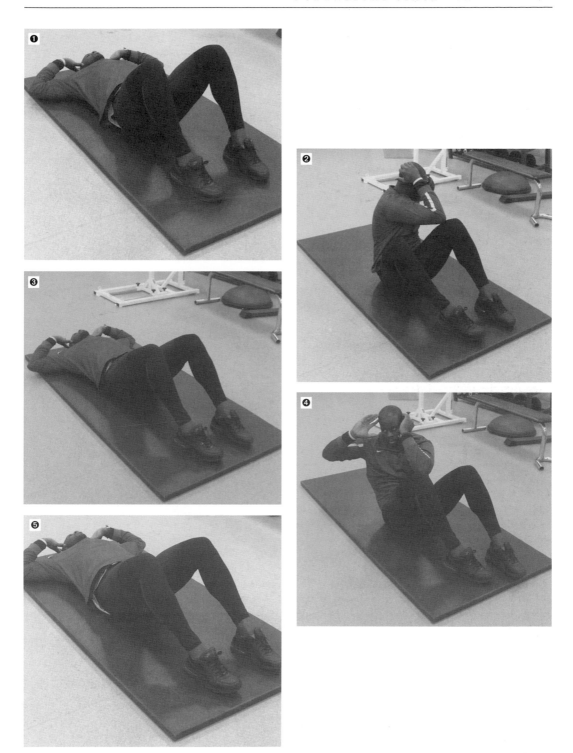

Figs 196, 197, 198, 199 & 200. Free twisting sit-ups.

The athlete lies on his or her back with the legs very slightly flexed (about 5–10 degrees); this is to protect the knee joints from hyperextension. The arms are laid alongside the body, and the feet either pointed up vertically in the neutral position or flat on the ground if this proves difficult. From here, the hips are lifted off the ground as far as possible and until the bodyweight is taken on the shoulders and heels. This position is maintained for 3sec, and the body then lowered slowly to the ground.

As athletes progress, the exercise becomes fairly easy, and so to make it more difficult a weight disc can be placed on the hips as a resistance.

The one-leg version of this is much more difficult, but is very effective in improving the core stability muscles. It should only be used with more experienced, and thus better conditioned athletes.

Free Twisting Sit-ups

Free twisting sit-ups are more effective than the simple straight version of the sit-up group of exercises, since they work the oblique and transverse muscle groups as well as the *rectus abdominis* group.

In the exercise the athlete lies on the ground with the legs bent to about 30

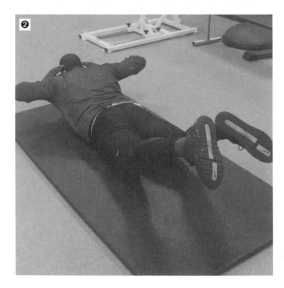

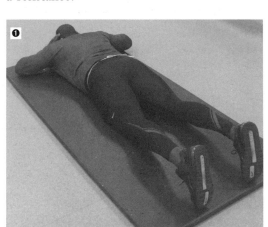

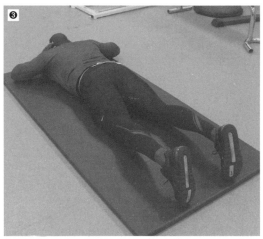

Figs 201, 202 & 203. Back hyperextensions.

degrees: sit-ups must never be performed with straight legs, as this puts maximum strain on the sacro-iliac and lumbar areas of the back. The hands are held close to the ears with the fingers lightly touching them; they must not be moved from here, as this would detract markedly from the effectiveness of the exercise.

From the horizontal position the body is curled up so that the head moves to the knees; as this is happening, the body is rotated to one side so that the elbow moves outside the opposite knee. It is important that this rotation is complete and smooth, as, again, any reduction in rotation will reduce the effect. From here the body is lowered under control back to the ground, and a second sit-up performed, this time to the other knee.

The exercise is surprisingly difficult, and often beginners find it hard to perform as their feet come off the ground; but with practice and increased strength it becomes more manageable.

Back Hyperextensions

(3sec hold)
This is perhaps the simplest and safest of the lower back exercises.

The athlete lies horizontal, face down, with the fingers of both hands under the chin or resting lightly at the side of the head behind the ears. The thighs and shoulders are lifted off the ground, and the position held for about 3sec. The body is then lowered under control.

A more difficult and effective version is the twisting back hyperextension, performed as above except that the shoulders are rotated to one side during each repetition, followed by the other side. This simple expedient of rotating during the hyperextension markedly increases the difficulty, but produces a far better result in terms of conditioning.

Chinnies

This is another mid-region exercise. It should not be confused with 'chins', in which exercise the body is pulled up to a beam with the arms.

Chinnies are performed starting with the body horizontal, face up, with the fingers held behind the ears, as for a sit-up. From here the body is curled towards one knee, and at the same time that knee is lifted to the outside of the oncoming elbow. It is vital that the whole movement is complete, because if it is not it becomes an easy but ineffective conditioning tool. The body is then lowered under control, and the movement repeated with the twist to the other knee. Once the athlete has mastered the rhythm it can be performed at speed, although technique should not be sacrificed under any circumstances.

Bench Dips

This is an excellent shoulder and triceps exercise.

The athlete supports him- or herself with the hands resting on a bench or chair with the feet on the ground. The lowering movement is effected by flexing the elbows, and is complete when the backside touches the ground. As a guide, the height of the bench or chair supporting the arms should be sufficient for the arms to reach complete flexion. Stronger athletes can perform this movement with both the hands and feet raised on benches or chairs. This makes the exercise considerably more difficult.

Beginners can, of course, use a shallower dip to get used to the movement, but ideally full range should be used.

Full-range Squat Jumps

This is a very effective leg-conditioning exercise, and works both the eccentric and concentric muscle actions. It must, however, be performed correctly, as balance difficulties can occur if strict technique is not observed. It is best done over the full range of leg flexion and extension, with the athlete crouching initially with the body as vertical as possible with the head facing forwards. From here, the legs drive the body

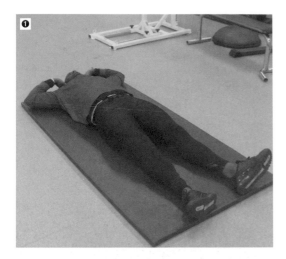

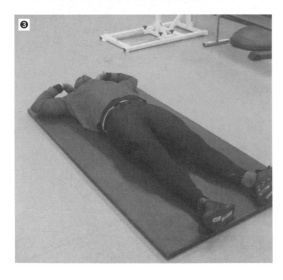

Figs 204, 205, 206, 207 & 208. Chinnies.

Figs 209, 210 & 211. Bench dips.

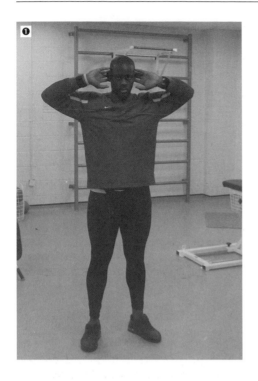

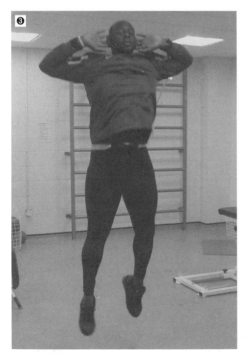

Figs 212, 213, 214 & 215. Full-range squat jumps.

upwards so that the feet come as far off the ground as possible. It is important to stress this full-range movement, because, in the same way as the other exercises, cutting it short reduces its efficacy.

For youngsters it is a good idea to make them touch the ground with both hands by the side of the body before jumping, and to throw the hands above the head while driving upwards. This teaches full extension in the jump. More experienced athletes should have the hands behind the head for the duration of the exercise.

The landing should be soft to absorb the shock, and the next repetition must be initiated without any delay in the movement. A rhythm can be built up which is the most economical way of performing a set of this exercise. If it becomes bitty and uncoordinated, it should be slowed down to regain control.

This session works most of the important muscles of the body, and more specifically those used in running and jumping.

THE ADVANCED SESSION FOR THROWERS

The following session is more applicable to throwers, and is essentially advanced in standard, with some tricky exercises in it.

Sample Session Structure

One Leg Supported Squats

This is a difficult exercise to learn, but, once the skill is there, it is a very good and unusual way of improving local muscular endurance in the quadriceps.

The athlete stands facing outwards from a bench, about 50cm from it. One leg is taken back and the foot rested on the bench. The hands are linked behind the head, and the body held in an erect position. The active leg is flexed, and the body lowered to the point where the bent knee is at about 90 degrees flexion. The leg is then straightened, and the body raised. Pressure on the rear leg should be at a minimum, and only sufficient to give stability to the movement. Great effort must be made to keep the body as close to vertical as possible by keeping the eyes looking forwards and the back tensed to keep it in position.

All the repetitions are completed on one leg, before changing to work the other.

Press-ups to Fingertips

This is performed in the same way as the press-up described above, except that at the end of the movement the athlete rises to the fingertips. This means that the arm drive must be much stronger and more dynamic

Suggested initial sets and repetitions:

1]	One leg supported squats	4 × 8 left / 8 right
2]	Press-ups to fingertips	4 × 10
3]	Leaning lunges	4 × 8 left / 8 right alternately
4]	Twisting, hanging knee tucks	4 × 6 left / 6 right alternately
5]	Bench back hyperextensions	4 × 10 (3 seconds hold at top)
6]	Alternate-leg 'V' sits	4 × 10 left / 10 right alternately
7]	Dips	4 × 10 (full range)
8]	Wide-stance split squat jumps	4 × 8 left / 8 right alternately

Fig 216, 217 & 218. One leg supported squats.

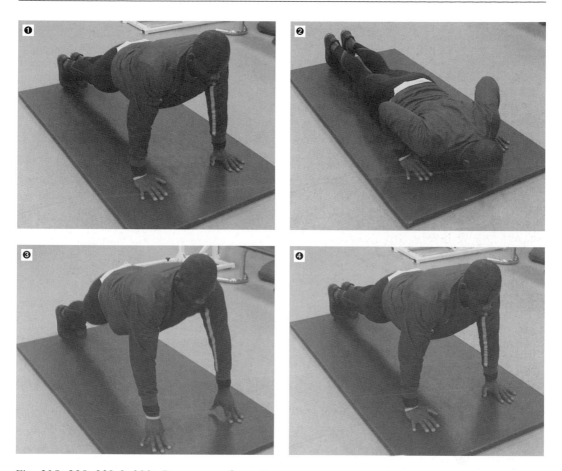

Figs 219, 220, 221 & 222. Press-ups to fingertips.

Figs 223, 224 & 225. Leaning lunges.

Figs 226, 227, 228, 229 & 230. Twisting, hanging knee tucks.

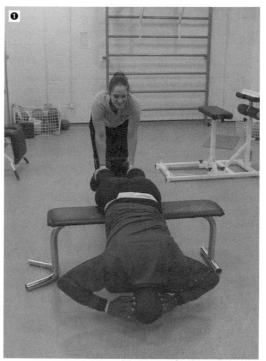

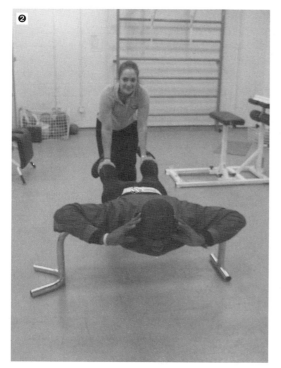

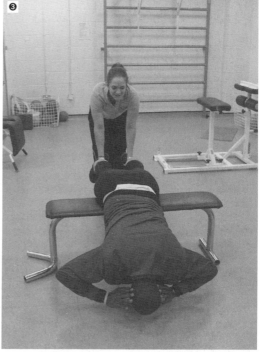

Figs 231, 232 & 233. Bench back hyperextensions.

than in the ordinary version, and care must be taken not to twist the hands and bend the wrists awkwardly. Its advantage over the normal version is that it co-ordinates all the chest and arm movements with those of the wrist and fingers. This relates to the deliveries in the shot put, discus and javelin throw, and helps with the hand grip of the hammer.

Leaning Lunges

This is another excellent single-leg exercise, and requires balance and strength to perform. The athlete adopts an upright standing position with the hands behind the head and the elbows facing outwards. The body is leaned forwards, while taking a long forward pace: this is achieved by keeping the rear leg straight. The movement stops when the abdomen reaches the thigh and the front leg is bent slightly beyond 90 degrees. From here the leg drives the body back up to its starting position, and the movement is repeated with the other leg forwards.

The athlete should attempt to keep the back leg and body in a straight line during the movement: this ensures that the back is not strained by too much backward lean during the initial part of the movement.

Twisting, Hanging Knee Tucks

This exercise requires a chinning bar and a pair of lifting wrist straps to perform well.

The athlete hangs free from the chinning bar, and straps his wrists to it. From a static position the knees are lifted to one side of the chest and held there for 2sec. They are then lowered under control, and lifted to the other side of the chest and held. It is important not to adopt a swinging motion to initiate the leg raise, as this negates the proper effect of the exercise.

Bench Back Hyperextensions

This is very similar to the flat back hyperextensions described above, except that the athlete initially lies horizontally, facing down with the hips on a bench and the feet held behind firmly and level with the hips. The hands are clasped behind the head, and the elbows held outwards for the duration of the exercise.

The body is then lowered, under control, until it reaches a position about 90 degrees to the horizontal. From here the back, held straight, is raised to a position just above horizontal, and held there for 2sec before repeating the movement. The athlete must not swing up violently, and must not lift the body more than a few degrees above the horizontal, as both of these can cause back injuries.

Alternate-leg 'V' Sits

This is an excellent and dynamic abdominal exercise.

The starting position is lying flat on the back with the arms stretched out beyond the head and touching, and the legs held straight, also touching. Simultaneously one leg and the torso are lifted towards each other to the point where the hands touch the toes of the rising leg. The athlete then resumes the starting position, and the other leg is raised with the body, and the toes touched.

Once the athlete has practised the movement a rhythm can be built up, and the whole exercise performed at speed. It is important, however, not to sacrifice technique by going too fast, and the toes must be touched in every repetition.

Dips

This is a very old exercise, but nevertheless an important addition to the list of activities essential to strength athletes. It requires a good pair of parallel bars, the distance between which should, if possible, be adjusted for each athlete.

To start, the athlete takes hold of the bars and jumps to arms' length, so he or she is supported on straight arms with the legs tucked underneath the backside. The head is held high, and the arms are fully bent so that the body is lowered under control. Once the lowest position has been reached the arms are vigorously extended to lift the body back up to the starting position.

Every effort must be made to keep the body from swinging, as this lessens the effect. Also the body should not be 'bounced' out of the low position as this can cause severe stress in the elbows. The exercise should be performed in controlled and smooth fashion.

Wide-stance, Split Squat Jumps

See p. 93 for a full explanation.

In Conclusion

The above session is complex and difficult to perform, but for the experienced athlete it can be challenging and interesting to do. As

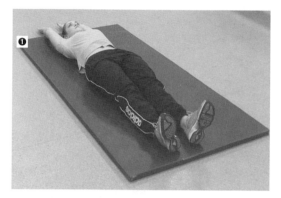

Figs 234, 235, 236, 237 & 238. Alternate-leg 'V' sits.

Figs 239, 240, 241 & 242. Wide-stance split squat jumps.

with all bodyweight stage training programmes, parts of the body become more tired than others. If there is a clear problem with a specific body segment, it is advisable to add extra exercises to put the emphasis on correcting the imbalances.

For young athletes, bodyweight training is particularly good for teaching how to use the body efficiently and effectively. Too often youngsters are put on to weight training before they can use the body properly, and this should not be done; a good guideline is for that athlete to be able to do twenty of each simple bodyweight exercise in perfect form before he or she lifts a weight. This will guarantee that the athlete will have sufficient natural strength to complete the often complex and difficult exercises involved in weight training.

SUMMARY

Bodyweight stage training is one of the very best methods for working on local muscular endurance, enabling the athlete to sustain complex movements without becoming too fatigued. It is also the starting point with circuits for young athletes who must learn to handle their bodies before they are subjected to the high stresses of weight training.

This type of training is infinitely variable, and, as well as being the core of local anaerobic exercise, it can also be used to supplement it. With a little thought, specificity can be integrated into each session, bringing interest and pertinence to the work.

CHAPTER 9

Medicine Ball Exercises

The medicine ball has been used in training from the earliest days of physical conditioning; many of the exercises were developed by the military as a means of strengthening and improving the fitness of recruits. From here the exercises moved into sport as an efficient way of improving athletes' performances, because the Services' fitness experts themselves moved into civilian life and transferred their knowledge into that sporting environment.

The great benefit of medicine ball work is that it can work either the whole body, or only specific parts, thus benefiting overall conditioning as well as core stability, in addition to being useful in resolving more localized problems. In terms of athletics, medicine balls have in particular been used by javelin throwers, basically because the athlete can approximate the throwing action using such resistance; this has led to many increasingly specific exercises being developed. However, the purpose of this book is to give a broad range of conditioning exercises, so we will concentrate on the more generally effective movements.

The basics of medicine ball work require that several different weights are available, since greater or lesser resistance will be needed, depending on the exercise to be performed. The best kind of ball is the inflatable rubber exterior type, as these are smaller and more easily manipulated than the leather alternatives.

As with all other forms of exercise, safety always comes first, and medicine balls can be dangerous if hurled at speed towards a person; this should never be allowed, and strict discipline must be applied during group activities.

The exercises to be described will be grouped according to the main body parts affected.

General exercises:
• Squat jump vertical throw
• Football throw-in
• Hammer-style throw
• Backward overhead throw

Chest, shoulder and arm exercises:
• Two-armed push
• Single-arm discus-style throw
• Seated throw-in
• Seated backward overhead throw
• Reverse one-arm triceps throw
• Lying vertical push (one- and two-arm)
• Lying throw-in
• Lying overhead backward throw

Mid-region exercises:
• Sit-up
• Sit-up throw-in
• Standing medicine ball circling
• Standing horizontal rotation
• Knee and leg raise
• Single- and double-leg kick

GENERAL EXERCISES

Squat Jump Vertical Throw

The ball is held in front of the face with the hands supporting it underneath. The legs are then bent so that the athlete squats down, but keeping the back upright and the ball firmly held in position. From here, he or she jumps upwards and then pushes the medicine ball vertically, thus combining the arm and

Figs 243, 244 & 245.
Squat jump vertical throw.

leg drive and making the whole body work during the movement. On landing the knees are bent to absorb the shock, and the ball is caught under control. The movement is then repeated. Do not try to do continuous repetitions unless the skill level is sufficiently high. Certainly to start with, perform one repetition at a time, focusing on accuracy of movement rather than maximum power.

As with all such exercises the skill requirement is high, and time is usefully spent on this before any power is applied.

Football Throw-in

This movement is performed in the same way as the football throw-in from the sideline, except of course that the medicine ball is much heavier than a football. The feet are spaced at shoulder width apart, and the ball is held overhead at arms' length with the

Figs 246, 247 & 248. Football throw-in.

hands to the rear of the ball. From here, the body is carefully arched back with minimal leg bend, and the ball moved behind the line of the body. The ball is then projected forwards by straightening the body using the abdominal muscles, and then throwing it with the arms. The feet are normally held on the ground to ensure stability.

This exercise is very good for general conditioning of the whole front body, as well as the shoulders and arms.

Hammer-style Throw

This exercise involves a movement similar to that used by the athletic hammer thrower. The ball is held in front of the body at waist height; the feet are spaced at shoulder width, and the knees are slightly bent. The ball is carried round to the right in a circular movement, at the same as bending the knees further. The head is held up, and the body bend kept to a minimum. From here the body is rotated to the left and the ball thrown upwards, extending the legs and body, two-handed, to the rear of the left side. The movement is then repeated, but turning in the opposite direction. This is to ensure balanced conditioning for both sides of the body.

This rotational movement uses both arms and legs. The link between the two, as in the previous exercises, is the mid-region, and it is these muscles that benefit most from this activity.

Backward Overhead Throw

This is the reverse of the 'football throw-in' exercise. The ball is held with two hands overhead, with the feet shoulder-width apart. The knees are then bent, and the ball taken down with the back straight to the front and between the knees. It is important to keep the head up, and not to flex the spine at this stage. From here the ball is flung backwards and up over the head at the same time as extending the legs so the trajectory is about 45 degrees. The feet should be kept fixed to the ground until the ball is released to maximize power and application of force.

This is an excellent exercise for explosive power, and in fact is often performed with metal shots, as are the above exercises. (In this instance, of course, the implements are not caught or thrown against a wall.)

CHEST, SHOULDER AND ARM EXERCISES

Two-armed Push

This exercise has many variations on a very simple theme, and the ball can be light or heavy depending on the objective. It is taken to the chest with the hands behind it and the elbows pointing outwards. The feet can either be placed as in normal standing, or with one foot in front of the other, the latter stance introducing a slight rotational stability requirement into the action. From here, the ball is pushed forwards and flicked off the fingers. It can be performed horizontally, upwards at an angle, or vertically. Working with a partner it can be performed rapidly over a short distance, or for power over a longer distance.

The main muscles used are the pushing muscles of the chest, shoulder, arms and wrist, working in a sequential movement similar to the shot-put delivery; however, it is not only that event that it benefits: it is also excellent for core stability in that the body must be held in a firm, controlled position to deliver the ball, and indeed to receive it.

The throw can also be performed against a wall, working on speed for movement and accuracy of catching.

Single-arm Discus-style Throw

This exercise requires the use of a small, light medicine ball, since the throw is one-handed. The feet can either be in a normal standing position, or with one in front of the other. The ball is taken in one hand at about waist height, and rotated backwards behind the body and then thrown with a sweeping movement to the front. The angle of delivery

Figs 249, 250 & 251. Single-arm discus-style throw.

can be varied according to need and to introduce variation.

The exercise works the rotational muscles of the mid-region as well as the anterior deltoids, pectorals and wrists. It must be performed with care and skill, and certainly when starting out a very light ball is best. The ball can be thrown against a wall to enable more repetitions to be performed, and to involve catching as well as throwing, thus increasing the work done.

Seated Throw-in

This is the same as the football throw-in, except that the athlete is seated on the ground. The exercise works the shoulders, triceps and forearm muscles, and requires good core stability to hold the body in position during the movement.

Figs 252, 253 & 254. Seated throw-in.

Seated Backward Overhead Throw
This again is the same as the standing version described earlier, except that the athlete sits on the ground to perform the movement. The exercise works the deltoids and upper back muscles effectively.

The action is difficult to perform, as the mid-region must take up all the movement required to deliver the ball. Initially, the athlete can experience difficulty with balance, but this soon improves with practice.

Figs 255 & 256. Seated backward overhead throw.

Figs 257, 258 & 259. Reverse one-arm triceps throw.

Figs 260, 261 & 262.
Lying vertical push
(one- and two-arm).

Figs 263, 264 & 265.
Lying throw-in.

Figs 266 & 267. Lying overhead backward throw.

Reverse One-arm Triceps Throw

This exercise is performed standing normally. The ball must be small and light, as it would be for most single-arm exercises. It is taken in one hand with the palm facing to the rear. It is then swung slightly to the front to initiate the movement, and then rapidly to the rear, working on attaining as much range as possible before releasing it. Every attempt should be made not to rotate the shoulders, as this introduces other muscles into the action.

This exercise works the rear shoulders, the wrists, and in particular the triceps.

Lying Vertical Push (One- and Two-arm)

This is performed with the athlete lying on the ground facing up. The ball is held in either one or two hands, the elbows pointing outwards with the palms facing upwards. The ball is then projected vertically upwards, and caught on its return to earth. This works the pushing muscles of the chest, shoulders, arms and wrists, isolating them from any body movement.

Care must be taken in performing this activity, as obviously the ball can land painfully if not under full control.

Lying Throw-in

This is similar to the standing and seated versions of the exercise. The athlete lies down on his or her back, face up, and takes the ball two-handed over the head to the arms-extended position. From here the athlete sits up and throws the ball overhead and forward. This movement works the abdominal muscles, shoulders, triceps and forearms.

Lying Overhead Backward Throw

This again is similar to the standing and sitting version of the exercise. With the athlete lying down, face up, the ball is taken in two hands to the waist. From here it is thrown up and over the head to the rear. This exercise works the back of the shoulders, the upper back and the forearms.

MID-REGION EXERCISES

This is where the medicine ball comes into its own, because, by its very nature, it can provide a versatile resistance to many and varied exercises that affect the core of the body.

Sit-up

The medicine ball can be used for all variations of the sit-up movement, including straight, twisting, inclined and hyper-extended. (This work is for experienced athletes who are capable of performing sit-ups easily, with no resistance.) The hyper-extended version should only be performed under supervision, and by those who are advanced in their experience.

The ball should be held to the chest so as to ensure a comfortable position, and to prevent putting too much pressure on the lower back. During the sit-up the back should remain curved forward, with the head slightly forward over the ball, and the knees bent. This will avoid injury and strain to the lower back.

Sit-up Throw-in

This is an advanced exercise that is difficult to perform well. The athlete lies on the ground, face up. The ball is held overhead at arms' length, and the knees are slightly bent. From here the athlete sits up and then throws the ball overhead and forwards. It is vital that the movement is done in that sequence, because if the ball is moved forwards before the sit-up, it makes the movement much easier but entirely useless.

This should not be tried by beginners or athletes who have lower back problems.

Standing Medicine Ball Circling

This is a straightforward but excellent exercise for the whole of the mid-region. It is performed standing up with the legs wide apart. The ball is held low in front of the body and at arms' length, and from here, it is taken in a circle for maximum range up above the head and then back to the low front position. The circle thus created should be as big as possible, and an equal number of circles should be performed in both directions to ensure balanced conditioning. As far as possible the movement should be smooth and flowing. This becomes easier once the athlete has become competent at performing it.

Standing Horizontal Rotation

This is an excellent exercise for improving rotational range of movement, as well as working the core stabilizer muscles. A medicine ball is held between the hands, with the elbows at 90 degrees to the body and tucked in; the body is then rotated to one side as far as possible, and held. After a second, a

Figs 268, 269 & 270. Sit-up.

Figs 271, 272 & 273. Sit-up throw-in.

Figs 274, 275, 276 & 277. Standing medicine ball circling.

Figs 278, 279 & 280. Standing horizontal rotation.

Figs 281 & 282. Medicine ball knee raise.

Figs 283 & 284. Medicine ball leg raise.

further twist is attempted to obtain maximum range. This final position is held for 3sec, then the body is rotated to the other side and a similar movement completed. It is important not to bend the knees, as this allows the hips to rotate, which nullifies the object of the exercise.

Medicine Ball Knee and Leg Raise

There is a variety of mid-region exercises that can be performed with medicine balls: these include variations on holding the ball between the feet or knees (with the legs bent and the back held flat to the ground to reduce possible back strain), and lifting the ball off the ground. This can be performed moving the legs vertically in a straight line, to either side or in a rotating manner. All of

Figs 285 & 286.
Medicine ball single-leg
kick.

these exercise the key core stability muscles, and are therefore a very useful adjunct to the sit-up/sit-back type of exercise.

A word of caution, though: these exercises require a good conditioning starting point, since, without reasonable core stability, the back cannot be held flat, and too much strain is placed on the lower back. Use these exercises only when you are sure the athlete can perform the movements correctly and safely.

Medicine Ball Single- and Double-leg Kick

When performed correctly, these exercises are a useful method for working the calves plyometrically, and with varied and controllable resistance. The athlete lies on his or her back, with the leg or legs bent and lifted off the ground about 1m. A partner then throws the medicine ball underarm and accurately, two-handed, on to the athlete's

Figs 287 & 288. Medicine ball double-leg kick.

toes, who responds by flicking it back using the calves. The legs must not be used, as this reduces the effect of the exercise on the calves. The movement must be controlled and reactive; a bouncing-type action is the best. It is not a push, but rather a flick of the foot or feet.

SUMMARY

There are many more exercises with medicine balls, some of them very specific to individual events. It is best to set up clear routines with set numbers of repetitions or time slots for each exercise; this way you will be able allocate finite training time to the work, and gauge improvement.

The problem with medicine ball work is that sessions are easy to do, but difficult to assess. It is therefore very important to conduct them precisely, so that some estimate of each athlete's abilities and improvements can be assessed.

Irrespective of these difficulties, medicine ball conditioning can be both enjoyable and hard work, giving the athletes varied and interesting, but testing routines that will produce great benefits without the tedium of standard gym sessions.

CHAPTER 10

Basic Strength Training and Planning

Strength is the athlete's means of increasing power. As we have seen, power is the result of combining speed with strength, and, as an athlete's basic inherent speed cannot be increased significantly, strength increase is the best and most significant way there is to improve power. Simply put, power equals speed, multiplied by strength. If speed can only be increased by, say, 10 per cent, then power will only advance by that amount. However, strength can usually be improved by up to 400 per cent from its base level: this means that, by working on strength and ignoring speed, power can be raised by a massive 400 per cent.

This, of course, is a simplistic way of viewing power, but in essence it guides us to an obvious conclusion: that strength training is a far more significant way of improving performance than simply by working on speed alone. The downside to this is that, as strength increases, so does bodyweight, and this will tend to reduce the effectiveness of the increased strength. In addition, as muscles grow in size during strength training, so the range of movement reduces – thus again having a negative effect on applicable power. However, these two negatives are not outweighed by the massive increases in strength that can be effected by proper strength training. (A detailed study of strength training is available in the companion book to this, *Strength Training for Athletes*, also published by The Crowood Press. In that book, the most important aspects of practical strength gain are detailed, with many examples of relevant exercises.)

In this chapter we will restrict ourselves to the basics, which should be known as a part of conditioning training for all athletes.

STRENGTH TRAINING AS PART OF THE YEAR PLAN

The athlete's year plan is the crux of his or her training. It starts with determining the most important competitions of the year, and sets the timescales of the peak periods needed to reach optimum performance. Each athlete is different, and the coach needs to experiment in the early years to see how long before reaching a peak the athlete needs to refine his or her training: some take two weeks, others five – it depends on the physical and psychological make-up of the athlete. In general I have used three weeks as an initial guideline, and then modified that time on the basis of experience. This is why it is vital that an athlete's diary is kept, because, from this, performance graphs can be drawn up that will indicate the preparation needed by each athlete.

Prior to the season at least a month of basic conditioning work will be needed, just to revitalize the athlete and to prepare him or her for the hard preparation work that will follow. Some athletes also need sharpening periods immediately before their peaks. These three phases – conditioning, sharpening and peaking – can all be mapped out from experience and need. Once this has been done, the strength gain phases can be placed in the gaps left available in the overall plan.

The number of attempted peaks during the year can also be varied, depending on the needs of the athlete and the dates of the major competitions. For example, a two-peak year is most often used so that the athlete reaches a first competitive peak in early new year (indoor season or cross-country/road race), followed by an outdoor track peak in the summer, early for non-international athletes and later for those who will be competing at the highest level.

Sometimes the competition structure is such that an athlete must qualify in mid-season and then compete at the major games late season. This can be encompassed within a three-peak year, namely early new year, mid-season, and then late season. This, however, is difficult to accomplish, and should only be attempted by very experienced athletes who can cope with the slight slump in performance between mid- and late season caused by returning to basic training at that time. Detailed plans must be made with the athlete on the basis of his or her experience, if the three-peak year is to be successful. Below are two sample year plans with the relevant periods marked in.

These sample plans should give an idea of a simple and effective way to plan the year, when to slot in the various training periods, and how to illustrate that plan in a clear way. Too many coaches prepare plans that are complex and difficult to understand: remember that the athlete wants to train, *not* study the intricacies of training theory.

In the plans below, the strength gain periods are marked as 'preparation' periods, and during the rest of the year – excluding the basic conditioning period at the start of the year – strength is maintained with at least one session of weights per week. As a guide-

Three-peak Year Plan

Month >	Oct	Nov	Dec	Jan	Feb	Mar	Apr	May	Jun	Jul	Aug	Sep
Period												
Conditioning	■											
Preparation 1		■	■	■								
Competition 1				■	■							
Preparation 2						■	■					
Sharpening 1								■				
Competition 2									■	■		
Intermediate 1											■	
Competition 3											■	■
Active Rest												■

Two-peak Year Plan

Month >	Oct	Nov	Dec	Jan	Feb	Mar	Apr	May	Jun	Jul	Aug	Sep
Period												
Conditioning	■											
Preparation 1		■	■	■								
Competition 1				■	■							
Preparation 2						■	■					
Sharpening 1								■				
Competition 2									■	■	■	
Active Rest												■

line, the throwers would be doing three weights sessions per week during preparation, the jumpers and power sprinters two, and the endurance athletes one. The strength training week plan for the various event groups might look as follows:

Endurance:

Monday	Heavy weights
Wednesday	Core stability and bodyweight session
Friday	Core stability and circuit training
Saturday	Core stability

Power sprints and jumps:

Monday	Heavy weights
Wednesday	Core stability and bodyweight session
Friday	Heavy weights
Saturday	Core stability

Throws:

Monday	Heavy weights
Wednesday	Power weights and core stability
Friday	Heavy weights
Saturday	Core stability and circuit training

Programming flexibility must be built into the schedule, since different athletes have different needs. Thus the schedule needs to be adaptable so it can accommodate the different rates of progress in individual athletes, their differing strengths and weaknesses, and also their injuries. As athletes progress over the years, the strength training balance must also change, towards more event-specific work. This is because strength can easily be maintained, and, like other forms of training, it reaches a point of diminishing returns as time progresses. Emphasis must therefore change to continue improvement in the later period of an athlete's career.

As a guideline, the following will give you an idea of how to plan the progress of an athlete over several years:

Age:		
16–19	General strength training	75 per cent
	Specific event strength training	25 per cent
19–22	General strength training	50 per cent
	Specific event strength training	50 per cent
22+	General strength training	25 per cent
	Specific event strength training	75 per cent

Should the athlete be starting later in life, then the boundaries are shifted accordingly with starting age and experience.

GENERAL STRENGTH EXERCISES

Every athlete needs to gain strength from their starting point. There are a number of universal exercises which, if used properly, will give the rapid all-round strength improvements required to improve power and performance during the competitive life of an athlete.

More coaches and athletes are realizing that 'fitness equipment', such as the 'multi-gym apparatus' and variations on that theme, are of only marginal effectiveness due to a lack of movement range and minimal skill requirement. There is no alternative to free weights, except for some very expensive equipment that is generally unavailable to the ordinary coach and athlete.

Below is a list of the 'must do' free weight exercises. More specific exercises can be added as required, but the following form the core of any athlete's programme:

1] Power clean
2] Power snatch
3] Back squat
4] Front squat
5] Squat to toes
6] Leg extension (normally performed using a suitable machine)

7] Leg biceps curl (normally performed using a suitable machine)
8] Bench press
9] Press behind neck
10] Arm biceps curl
11] Lat pull down (normally performed using a suitable machine)
12] Bent-over rowing
13] Upright rowing

Power Clean

The power clean is the easiest general exercise to perform, and consists simply of lifting the barbell from the ground and catching it on the shoulders. The movement is often made complicated beyond recognition, but essentially it is quite simple. The barbell is placed on the ground, and the athlete stands with the feet under the bars as far as the insteps, and about shoulder-width apart. He or she then sits down towards the bar with the head up and the back straight (not vertical), and slightly leaning forwards so that the bar can be grasped comfortably. This grip is slightly wider than shoulder-width, and comfortable.

From here the back is tightened, the eyes keep looking forwards, and the legs straighten slightly before the back, as the bar is lifted. As the weight accelerates upwards, brushing or even hitting the thighs, the arms are brought into action to pull the moving bar up to the shoulders. As it reaches the shoulders the hands are flipped over so the bar lands on the deltoids with the elbows forced up and forwards to stabilize the position. The knees should be bent slightly to assist the wrist turn and absorb the shock of receiving the bar. This, however, should be minimal, and athletes should not attempt the very difficult squat catching position – unless, of course, they are set on competing in weightlifting.

The sequence of applying power is legs, back, arms and then wrists, and this sequence is vital for the most efficient way of lifting the bar to the shoulders. The exercise works virtually all the muscles of the active body, and is the key to developing linear core

Figs 289, 290 & 291.
Power clean.

stability; nevertheless good technique is essential for maximum benefit. A long period of skill training is important, and in itself teaches co-ordination and balance.

Power Snatch

This is similar to the power clean, except that the bar is pulled above the head at arms' length. The starting position is close to that for the clean, except that the hand grip is much wider in order to reduce the eventual height to which the bar must be lifted. In one way this makes the exercise easier, but in another more difficult, because the wide grip necessitates a lower starting position and a more difficult wrist angle with which to apply the force.

Figs 292, 293, 294 & 295. Power snatch.

To gain the best results, no dip should be used to catch the bar; rather, complete extension of legs, body and arms should be attempted. This makes the exercise much more difficult and less weight can be used, but it is also a more effective exercise. There is no need to use very heavy weights to gain much from this highly skilful exercise.

Back Squat

This is *the* basic leg extending strengthening exercise, but it also has considerable benefi-cial effects on the hamstrings, adductors, gluteals and the lower back. It is performed by holding the bar on the back of the shoulders (not the neck) in a comfortable position. The head is held up with the eyes focused for the whole lift on a point in front and level with the eyes. The back is tightened and straight (not necessarily vertical), and the feet are placed ideally no wider than the shoulders, and slightly turned out. It is easier to perform with the feet wider, but its effects become less significant the more they are moved away from the normal standing position.

Figs 296, 297 & 298. Back squat.

Fig 299. Front squat.

Some athletes have hereditary stiff ankles and can be allowed to put small discs or a piece of wood under the heels. However, most should be able to full squat comfortably with the feet flat; if this is not the case, some effort must be made to correct the suppleness problem before serious squatting is attempted.

From the initial position the knees are bent carefully and steadily until the top of the thighs are parallel with the ground. A lower depth is unnecessary for athletes, and should not be attempted. From the low position the legs drive the weight up to the starting position; the movement is then repeated the required number of times. Two reliable 'spotters' should always be in place when heavy weights are attempted near failure level.

Front Squat

This exercise requires the athlete to hold the bar on the front of the shoulders either in clean catch position, or on the anterior deltoids, with the hands resting facing downwards on the bar to stabilize the position. It subtly moves the centre of gravity forwards, so the body must be held in a more vertical position during the squat and drive up. This means that the exercise affects the front quadriceps much more than the back squat,

Figs 300, 301, 302 & 303. Back squat jump.

an advantageous effect for athletes who tend to use this part of the leg more than the upper thigh during their events.

It is, however, more difficult to perform, and some time practising the movement with light weights is of benefit, to ensure confidence of movement.

Back Squat to Toes, and Back Squat Jump

This exercise is merely an extension of the back squat, in which the athlete drives on to the toes at the end of the squat. In addition it works the calves, and thus the co-ordination of the sequential muscle usage is extended to include those muscles. It is therefore more 'complete' in terms of working all the leg-driving muscles.

Leg Extension

(Normally performed using a suitable machine.)

This, and the leg biceps curl, are the only leg exercises that need to use machinery in their performance. The leg extension starts with the athlete sitting upright with the back held upright, and the weight comfortably across the upper insteps of the feet. The position is held firm by holding the bench or the support grips at the sides.

The quadriceps are then contracted so that the weight moves in an arc up to the horizontal. For maximum effect it is essential that the legs are held straight for 2–3sec once they reach this position, and before the weight is lowered to its starting position. This is to eliminate any swinging action, which makes

 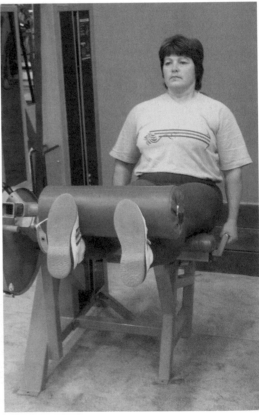

Figs 304 & 305. Leg extension.

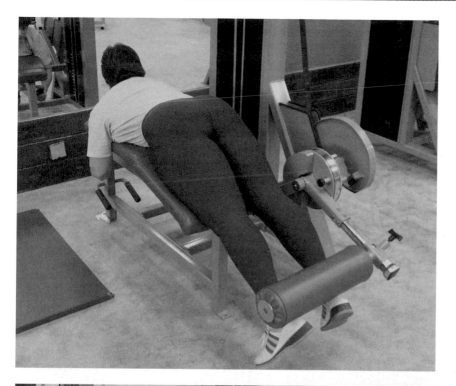

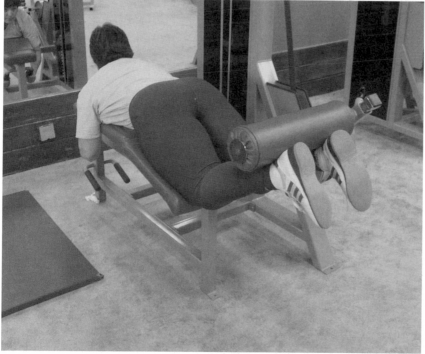

Figs 306 & 307. Leg biceps curl. (*Continued overleaf.*)

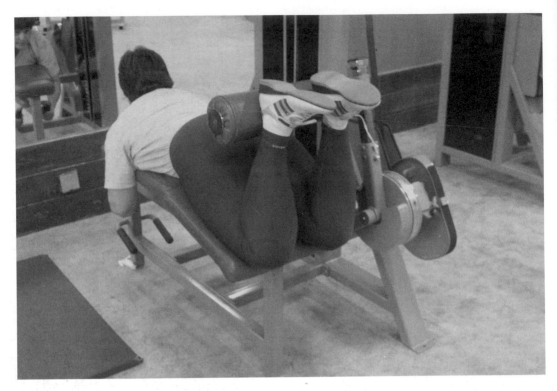

Fig 308. Leg biceps curl.

the exercise considerably easier to perform and much less effective. In addition, the weight must come to a complete halt between repetitions in order to prevent swinging.

This is an excellent exercise for developing quadriceps strength, but some athletes can find it painful on the knees; if this is the case it should be avoided, as it can increase any underlying injury.

Using lighter weights it can also be used effectively for quadriceps rehabilitation after a knee operation or other leg problem. In these cases the exercise can be performed on each leg individually, giving a means of comparing the relative strengths of the two legs, a useful indicator for assessing the progress of rehabilitation.

Leg Biceps Curl

(Normally performed using a suitable machine.)

The leg biceps curl works the hamstrings very effectively, and is the only exercise in which the resistance can be quantitatively varied. It is, however, vital that it is performed strictly and over the fullest possible range, because, if it is not, shortening of the hamstring can cause severe problems during most athletic events.

There are good and bad machines on which to perform the exercise; the best consist of a slightly arched-up bench and adjustable positioning for the weight pads. This is vital, since the force should be applied through the heels, and not the calves, to prevent damage to the Achilles tendons. It is also important to make sure that the fulcrum (pivot point) at the knees is correctly placed to ensure an accurate path of movement.

The exercise should be performed from an absolutely straight-legged starting point. From here, the legs are slowly bent to around 90 degrees, and then slowly straightened back

Figs 309, 310, 311 & 312. Bench press.

to the starting position. The whole movement must be controlled and not rushed; also the legs must not be flexed maximally, as this will often induce cramp when fatigue starts to set in.

Despite its difficulty, the leg biceps curl is an excellent exercise for both strengthening and rehabilitating the hamstrings. Each leg can be worked individually, as with the leg extension, so that comparative strengths between the legs can be simply assessed.

Bench Press

The bench press is one of the landmark exercises, in the same way as the power clean, power snatch and back squat. It is often used as a basic measure of arm and chest strength, particularly by throwers.

It is performed by the athlete lying on the back, face up, on a bench with the feet firmly placed flat on the ground and the back slightly hyperextended to give a firm and

Figs 313 & 314. Press behind neck.

controlled starting position. A barbell is held at arms' length over the upper chest, with the hand grip such that the arms are vertical. Wider grips tend to be used only when more emphasis on the pectoral muscles is required. The bar is then lowered slowly and under control to the sternum. As soon as it touches, the arms are vigorously extended back to the starting position.

The athlete will take a deep breath before lowering the bar, and will hold it until near the finishing position, at which point he or she will exhale. This is to give a firm ribcage over which the pectoral muscles can operate more efficiently.

Although a light bounce is permissible, heavy bouncing can lead to injury and should be avoided.

The exercise mainly works the pectoral, anterior deltoid and triceps muscles, but it also involves the core stability muscles in the maintenance of posture.

Press Behind Neck

This is a difficult exercise to perform with heavy weights, and it needs plenty of practice with a light resistance to perfect the technique.

The athlete may stand or sit. The barbell is placed on the back of the shoulders, and

Figs 315, 316 & 317. Arm biceps curl.

the upper body is held firm and erect; if the standing version is being performed the legs are locked. From here, a deep breath is taken, as in the bench press, and the bar is pushed to a position above the head with the arms fully extended. Balance becomes more difficult as the bar rises, so it is important that the starting position is very stable.

The bar is then lowered carefully back to the shoulders. Great care must be taken not to drop the bar on the back of the neck as this can cause damage to the small vertebrae of that region. If necessary the legs can be bent to absorb the shock of returning the bar, and if necessary spotters can be used if the weight is near maximum and control is difficult.

Arm Biceps Curl

This is an exercise beloved of body builders, who often put a great emphasis on the size of the upper arm. Even so, it is still a useful exercise to counterbalance the arm-pushing work done in the bench press and the press behind neck exercises, because it works the forearms and biceps muscles.

The basic exercise is performed standing erect, with the legs and body locked into position. The barbell is held at arms' length resting on the thighs, the grip being such that the arms are parallel. After taking a deep breath, the bar is then 'curled' up towards the chin by contracting the biceps and forearm muscles. The finishing position should be somewhat short of the chin. This is to ensure that the elbow joint is not strained, because at this point the bar can force the joint open purely by virtue of its weight, and cause severe elbow strain.

The bar is then lowered carefully to its starting position, with arms fully extended. This is important, because, if the whole arm flexion range is not exercised, the biceps tend to shorten and the athlete starts to resemble an ape with permanently bent arms.

Lat Pull Down

(Normally performed using a suitable machine.)

Figs 318, 319 & 320. Lat pull down (wide grip to back of shoulders).

Figs 321, 322 & 323. Lat pull down (narrow grip to chest).

Figs 324, 325 & 326. Bent-over rowing (wide grip to chest).

Figs 327, 328 & 329. Bent-over rowing (narrow grip to abdomen).

This is a most useful basic exercise to counterbalance the spine-compressing exercises such as the back squat. The athlete sits on a bench: for the wide grip to back of shoulders version he or she faces away from the machine; for the narrow grip to chest version of the exercise he or she faces the machine.

The wide-grip version works the *latissimus dorsi* and arm biceps muscles, while the narrow-grip version works mainly the biceps and posterior deltoids. Both are good exercises and can be performed alternately week on week to ensure good muscular balance in the upper body.

The starting position is with the bar gripped above the head with the arms fully extended; this initial extension is important for the same reasons as in the biceps curl. From here, the bar is pulled down to the back of the shoulders or the front of the chest, as the exercise requires; it is then returned under control to the starting position.

Bent-over Rowing

Bent-over rowing is one of the few exercises that works the upper back, and is another good counterbalance to arm-pushing exercises such as the bench press. It can be performed with heavy weights, as long as the skill has been learnt before heavy weights are used.

The bar is placed on the ground and the athlete stands with knees slightly bent and back straight, and then leans forward over the bar, which should be below the chest. A wide grip is taken on the bar, and the posture firmed up to avoid any bend in the back during the movement. The bar is then pulled steadily up to the chest, and returned to the ground. Great care must be taken not to jerk the bar up, as this will put considerable strain on the lower back.

A narrow-grip version can also be performed, in which the hands are placed on the bar so that the arms are vertical. From here the bar is pulled to the abdomen. This exercise works slightly lower back muscles, and can be used as a variation.

Upright Rowing

This is an excellent postural exercise, working mainly the upper back and posterior deltoid muscles. A good solid standing position is adopted, and the bar gripped with the hands about 15cm apart, and at arms' length. From here the bar is pulled with the elbows uppermost, to the chin.

There must be no swinging or backward arching, and at the final position the bar must be as high as possible under the chin. The bar is then lowered back down to arms length, and the exercise repeated. For the exercise to be most effective the elbows must be kept above the hands right up to completion of the movement.

SETS AND REPETITIONS

The heavier the weight used, the more strength is needed to move the bar, and the fewer repetitions can be performed. This will give the highest levels of strength gain. At the other end of the spectrum, the lighter the weight and the higher the repetitions, the more aerobic the activity becomes. In between lies a range of mixed effects. The simple diagram on p. 161 defines the effects of different weight-training sets and repetitions.

Using these guidelines to set the sets and repetitions for your conditioning training will allow you to determine the effect it will have.

Designing the Sessions

For general strength conditioning the sessions should be designed to work the whole body. I have found the sequence on p. 161 most satisfactory for athletes of all ages.

The exercises in which weights are used are progressed by increasing the weight once the full sets and reps have been achieved: this is called progressive resistance training, and is at the heart of strength gain. Only keep the weight the same if technique is being worked on at the early stage. The exercises that do not use weights are progressed by increasing

Figs 330, 331 & 332. Upright rowing.

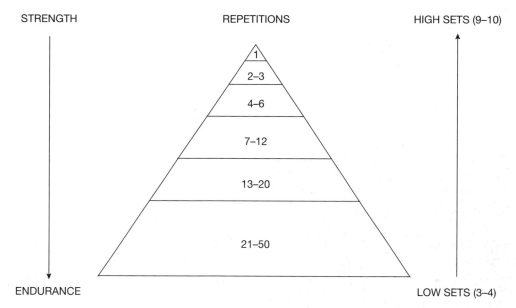

Relationship between sets, repetitions and strength/endurance effect during weight training

Exercise		
1	All-round body exercise (power cleans or snatches)	4 × 10
2	Arm-push exercise (bench presses or presses behind neck)	4 × 10
3	Arm-pull exercise (biceps curls or lat pull downs)	4 × 10
4	Abdominal-curl exercise (sit-ups or crunches)	4 × R/R
5	Back-curl exercise (flat or bench back hyperextensions)	4 × R
6	Second abdominal-curl exercise (alternate-leg 'V' sits or chinnies)	4 × R/R
7	Leg-push exercise (back or front squats)	4 × 10
8	Leg jumping exercise (squat jumps or alternate leg split jumps)	4 × 10
9	Calf exercise (bounce jumps or supported bounce jumps)	4 × 20

the repetitions (R or R/R above where 'R' is the number of repetitions performed for a single-sided exercise, and 'R/R' is the number of repetitions performed each side for a double-sided exercise); this will ensure steady improvement over the length of the training period.

(More detailed explanations and many examples of exercises are included in the companion book to this edition, *Strength Training for Athletes*, also published by The Crowood Press.)

SUMMARY

Strength training is the most important and effective way for the athlete to increase power, and it is therefore vital that the coach sets programmes that will give maximum results in the minimum time. Strength training is essentially simple, and there are many ways to make the work enjoyable, and not tedious. The most important element is for the athlete to see that he or she is improving: this is great motivation. However, it must be explained that strength gains do not give immediate improvements in the events; it takes some time for the co-ordination to adapt to the new power levels. If the general strength work is planned properly, and the sessions designed to suit the event needs, then progress can be made for many years until the athlete needs no more general strength and tends towards more specific exercises.

The most important aspect of strength that the coach needs to appreciate is that the body will return to its original, or near-original strength levels if the work is not maintained. To maintain these levels requires only one heavy weight session per week – but not doing this for any length of time will lead to diminishing power, and therefore less chance of competitive improvements. It is important to use common sense: for instance, if an athlete is in the last weeks leading up to a competition, it is only the heavy throwers who need to maximize this maintenance. Athletes in other events can ease off, as long as the heavy work restarts immediately after the competition.

Different athletes respond and recover in different ways, and I strongly advise coaches to find out how close to a maximum event effort the athlete can go with the heavy weight session. There is a surprising variation, as some athletes like to feel strong, while others like to feel loose. Strength training is a vital part of an athlete's progress, so the coach must gain as much knowledge as possible to ensure success.

CHAPTER 11

Specific Event Conditioning

The heading of this chapter might seem to be a paradox, since conditioning is normally accepted as being general training to prepare the athlete for the specifics of the event. In the early days when conditioning was developed as an adjunct to event work, this was the case, but now training has moved so far that even what we might consider to be general conditioning has a specific edge to it.

Taking long distance and discus as examples, it is clear to us all that, in spite of the inclusion of similar elements at the most basic level, virtually all the work done will be geared towards the development of the abilities required for the event. This is because we now understand the physiological basis of each event, and can fast-track the athlete's development by avoiding all the work that would have minimal influence. In addition, the right balance of training methods can be introduced very early in an athlete's career. Obviously, this depends on the coach knowing enough about the event and the requirements of the event: analysis of the athlete and the event is therefore the starting point for all training programme planning.

EVENT ANALYSIS

It does not take a genius to realize that the long-distance runner does not do heavy weight training all year round, or the hammer thrower cross-country running. But understanding the detail of the physiological requirements of each event is a difficult and time-consuming affair. Nevertheless, these days it is not possible to be a top-level coach without the knowledge and ability to analyse the event as well as the athlete.

Event analysis involves looking at the basic physiological, physical and psychological needs of the event, and being able to design the schedule with these very much in mind. Coaches often work with groups of athletes, and many give them the same work regardless of their event and ability – to develop the schedules in line with the individual athletes is hard work and requires considerable determination on the part of the coach to put into practice; it is much easier to make everyone do the same thing. But progress will be short-lived if this approach is maintained, and it is not surprising that these coaches are left wondering what happened in the later years of an athlete when early success seemed so easy.

TRAINING SPECIFICITY

The specific work requirement increases the longer an athlete trains, and it is this assessment that lies at the heart of moving an athlete all the way up the scale to full international and world-class performance.

In the previous chapter it was suggested how the general and specific strength should vary over the lifespan of an athlete, but this is also true for the other conditioning work elements. Basically, as the athlete gets older and more skilled, the only avenue for improvement lies within the event-specific content of the sessions. For example, at an early stage a simple basic circuit might suffice to produce excellent aerobic and anaerobic improvement in all athletes, but later on this is not only too easy for the athlete, but its effect peaks quite quickly. It would therefore be prudent to move the exercises more towards those of the event, as this will initiate and maintain adaptation of the body in closer alignment to those movements. Thus sprint-arm action might replace press-ups for the runners, and one-arm dumb-bell press or swing might replace press-ups for the throwers.

Specific Suppling

A specific aspect can be developed for all the conditioning elements; it is largely a matter of adopting the mind-set of the event in relation to the element being considered. Suppling and mobility are a basic and similar requirement of all events, and it would seem that little can be devised from these that is not of a general nature. Nevertheless, each event needs at least some small variation in range and direction of movement.

The simplest is, of course, long-distance running, which involves minimal range of movement to ensure the economy of action that is essential to maximize metabolic efficiency. It would be strange indeed to see a marathon runner striding out in the same way that an 800m runner or sprinter does – in fact it would be positively detrimental to performance to do this. On the other hand, the hurdler has a complex and rangy movement to perform in clearing the obstacles, with the trail leg needing to operate at 90 degrees to the normal running position: without some specific suppling, this action would be difficult indeed. This also applies to the javelin thrower, whose throwing arm just prior to delivery causes the joints to operate at the extreme range of mobility: considerable time must thus be taken in ensuring the maximum suppleness of the soft tissue to prevent serious injury to the shoulder and elbow.

It is clear that the athlete needs to ensure sufficient suppleness to be able to approach the maximum mobility, and therefore joint range, that is required by the event. Simply continuing to condition in a general way throughout the athlete's career will limit the possibilities for certain events.

A word of caution, however: some coaches make their athletes do much suppling, and it is possible that this can have a deleterious effect on the joints and soft tissues. The rule of thumb should be to aim for sufficient suppleness to allow the athlete to perform the required movement with ease.

Specific Core Stability

Observation of athletes performing jumping events will convince any coach that core stability is a most important element. But not all events require the same maintenance of position under such extreme physical pressure. The triple jumper is at the extreme end of this requirement, as the forces are so great that many jumpers simply cannot jump at flat-out speed because the posture collapses at that level of effort. This would imply that a great deal of specific core stability work is an essential part of a jumper's programme.

Most other events do not have this high stability requirement, or at least do not need to maintain it under such pressure. It is more important for the runner to be able to maintain good posture for long periods of time, rather than being able to resist high forces for a short period. Even the sprint events that have to withstand the high forces of the start, and the acceleration phases of their events, will find that endurance-based core stability is more a part of being able to perform well in training than competing in a one-off race. This also applies to the throwers, who need a certain amount of specific core stability work related to their throwing actions, but who also need endurance work, which must not be neglected as it enables many repetitions of the movement to be performed without fatigue.

As a general recommendation, then, it would appear that core stability needs to be maintained generally in its normal endurance-based format, but additional work for the event is required, as the athlete needs to improve the application of force within the event.

Specific Aerobic Conditioning

The only specific aerobic conditioning necessary in any event is that for the endurance events, where this type of conditioning is actually the heart of the event-specific training. General basic aerobic conditioning is adequate for all the other events.

Specific Anaerobic Conditioning

All running events require specific anaerobic conditioning to a greater or lesser degree: the sprints have a very high component, endurance less so, and long distance minimal. This is, again, part of the normal event-specific training, and as such cannot be categorized as anything separate. All of the jumps require additional running anaerobic conditioning to allow the athlete to train at the highest level for extended periods.

The throws need only basic anaerobic conditioning but can benefit from some local muscular endurance work in specifically poor areas. Local muscular endurance is anaerobic fitness in local areas of the body such as the arm and shoulder in discus and javelin, the triceps and wrist in shot put, and the back in hammer. All these isolated areas come under more stress than any other part of the body in terms of fatigue, and will benefit from extra, specific anaerobic conditioning in the gymnasium.

Specific Speed and Power

Speed and power seem to be highly specific to a movement. For example, a fast cyclist is not necessarily a fast sprinter, and a fast shot putter is not necessarily a fast swimmer. It is therefore important that fast conditioning for power or to maintain basic speed is more related to the events.

The more technical the event, the more specific is the speed element of the movement. As the athlete progresses it is therefore important to start introducing speed- and power-related exercises that enhance, rather than detract from, the actions involved in the event. The exercises used in the sessions described in the chapter on speed and power can be refined as the athlete gains experience, to the point when 'special power' conditioning can be employed effectively. This relates to the 'special strength' work that many athletes do, which is using an activity forming part of the actual athletic event against an increased resistance. When using light additional resistances, the work improves mainly power; when they are heavy they improve strength, although this tends to interfere somewhat with the application of power.

This may seem confusing, but, taking the discus throw as an example, it has been found that throwing a heavy discus has a positive direct effect on power only as long as the weight does not exceed the normal implement weight by more than 10 per cent. Once it goes above this, the technique is modified to counterbalance the increased weight, and the effect becomes less specific. The way round this is to do simpler movements, such as a standing throw, rather than the turn with heavier implements. The resulting effect seems then to be more beneficial in terms of power, even if it is in only part of the event. It is a similar scenario for the sprinters, in that running against a resistance alters the technique if the resistance is too great, and can therefore become counterproductive.

In summary, event-specific speed and power training becomes more important the more technical the event. However, to ensure that the techniques of the events are not disturbed by special power conditioning, only light (plus 10 per cent) resistances should be employed.

Specific Circuit and Bodyweight Stage Training

Circuit and bodyweight stage training is normally considered an alternative way of working aerobically and anaerobically, and, by making the exercises progressively more specific over a period of years in the athlete's programme, the rule of increasing specificity can be adhered to. In addition, specificity in the sessions can be a useful tool in honing the mental focus for a competition.

Most exercises can be modified to incorporate a more specific element with a little thought: for example, change squat jumps for narrow-stance split squat jumps for the runners; and try leaning forward lunges instead of squat thrusts for the throwers, and step-up drives instead of calf jumps for the jumpers. Furthermore, if an athlete has a specific technical problem, try designing the session to work that particular aspect harder: not only will such modifications be directly beneficial, they will also add purpose for the athlete.

Specific Strength Conditioning

This sort of conditioning has been referred to in an earlier chapter. Suffice it to say that such work is as vital as the specific speed and power training, but it does not have the same restraints because a perfect closeness to the event technique is not being sought.

'Special strength' conditioning – involving the use of heavy resistances during event movements – can be performed with success if it is not too close to a period of high-quality training or competition. It is advisable to use such activities in the preparation periods only, with emphasis on 'special speed and power' work closer to competition. In this way any technical adaptations made during the heavy work can be corrected during the light phase.

As the athlete moves along the path of his or her athletic career, specific and special strength becomes an increasingly important part of training. It is therefore a good idea to introduce the concept at an early age, because in this way the athlete will naturally gravitate to its use smoothly, over a period of years.

SUMMARY

Specific conditioning is at the heart of the training programme for all athletic events. To a greater or lesser degree, even if the athlete is technically superb, he or she can benefit from such work in the neverending quest to reach potential. Event analysis, imagination and thought are essential prerequisites for the coach in designing and planning the specific conditioning elements of the programme, and need to be viewed as a multi-year project.

There is, of course, no substitute for basic conditioning, and it must be said that this must be the initial focus of the programme; but, as the athlete develops, specific work becomes more and more relevant to attaining that last inch of improvement that makes the difference between success and failure.

CHAPTER 12
Conclusion

Within this book and its companion, *Strength Training for Athletes*, is much sensible advice on the training of athletes. There are many ways to address the problems that the coach encounters during his or her quest to enable athletes to reach as close to their potential as possible. The methods described are not exhaustive: rather, they are common-sense answers to how to achieve good results with the majority of athletes.

The 'icing on the cake' must come from the inspiration of the coach and the support team, whose overall responsibility is to learn, and to keep learning, about the individual, and what makes him or her 'tick'. By combining all these factors, a satisfactory result can always be achieved. It is only when the basics are ignored or simply not followed that problems occur.

Always apply simple common sense to a problem; resolution often comes from a re-examination of the training programme and the basic conditioning that has been attempted. Small errors can build up over the years, so it is vital that difficulties are picked up early. To this end, regular testing and recording are an essential part of the athlete's training.

Finally, remember that conditioning is the way to guarantee balanced improvement. At the end of his or her career the athlete must return to normal life, and he or she will not thank you for any damage that persists into their future life. While it is equally the responsibility of the athlete to report problems, it is the good coach who can quickly recognize them almost before they arise, and will stop and modify a programme accordingly. Never be afraid to say you have got it wrong: if you can do this, the mistakes will not be compounded by an inability to admit the truth. Coaches are, after all, human and fallible.

Glossary

Active suppling Form of suppling in which external pressure is applied to increase range of movement.

Adenosine tri-phosphate (ATP) The main energy-rich biochemical formed during aerobic and most anaerobic activities.

Aerobic activity Activities based on energy production using oxygen.

Alveoli Tiny air sacs that are at the ends of the tiniest branches of the lungs' airways, and in which the gases are exchanged between the air and the blood.

Anaerobic (long term) Exercise performed flat out for 45–50sec, usually producing high levels of lactic acid.

Anaerobic (short term) Flat-out physical exercise lasting no more than 8–12sec, using residual stores of creatine phosphate as the energy supply.

Anaerobic activity Activities based on energy production not using oxygen.

Biochemical Related to the chemistry of all living things.

Biochemical pathways Series of biochemical reactions involved in converting one substance to another (others).

Bodyweight training Exercise routines involving only the athlete's own bodyweight.

Bounding A running-type movement involving very high knee lift and extra long stride length.

Calories 1 calorie = the energy needed to heat 1g of water by 1°C.

Capillary Smallest blood vessel in the body where gases and chemicals are exchanged.

Circuit training Training in which a series of exercises are performed in a series starting with one set of the first and finishing with the last before going back to the beginning.

Conditioning The physical techniques used by athletes to prepare generally and specifically for individual events.

Core The part of the body connecting the thorax (chest) to the legs, otherwise known as the mid-region.

Creatine phosphate (CP) A biochemical used in cells as a reservoir of easily available energy.

Depth jumping Jumping off and reacting on landing, from platforms or boxes of varying heights.

Enzyme Protein in the cell that speeds up biochemical reactions.

Erythropoetin (EPO) Natural hormone produced in the kidneys, which increases the number of red blood cells in the blood.

Explosive activity One-off maximum-speed and -effort activities such as the release in throwing events or standing jump.

Fartlek training Form of training in which fast running is regularly interspersed with slow recovery running.

Glycolysis Biochemical reactions that break down glucose into smaller compounds (during aerobic energy production).

Hydrogen ion transfer The last process in aerobic energy production where the products of the Krebs' cycle are used to produce ATP.

Hyperextension of a joint Range of movement beyond normal extension.

Hypertrophy The increase in muscle size noticed after a period of heavy weight training.

Isometric activities Activities involving the application of force, but which produce no movement.

Krebs' cycle Cyclical series of biochemical reactions that break down small products of glycolysis with the aid of oxygen to produce high-energy compounds.

Lactic acid The main (poisonous) by-product of anaerobic activity.

Maximum single repetition A weight training term defining the maximum resistance able to be used in performing one repetition of an exercise.

Medicine ball Soft, weighted rubber ball between 15 and 30cm in diameter.

Medulla oblongata The part of the brain between the cerebellum and the spinal cord, from which most of the basic bodily functions, such as breathing, are controlled.

Mitochondrion Small ovaloid part of a cell that is concerned with aerobic energy production.

Mixed sessions Training in which several different conditioning elements are performed in a single session.

Mobility The range of movement allowed by the joints.

Muscle-bound The bodily state in which the muscles are so big that they radically reduce range of movement.

Muscle contraction Shortening of muscle(s), which produces force and hence movement.

Muscle fibre The fibre-like functional unit of voluntary muscle.

Muscle tone The state of readiness of a muscle to contract.

Neuro-muscular pathways The bodily pathway from the brain, along the motor nerves to the muscles.

Oxidative processes Biochemical reactions in the cells involving the 'burning' of carbohydrates and fats with oxygen, to produce energy.

Passive suppling Form of suppling in which no external pressure is applied to increase range of movement.

Physical elements of conditioning The different parts of conditioning based on the physiology of the athlete.

Plyometric activity Reactive activity such as long-jump take-off.

PNF Proprioceptive neuro-muscular facilitation: a form of suppling involving contraction of the antagonist muscles prior to stretching.

Power The mathematical product of strength multiplied by speed.

Preparation training The training conducted by the athlete leading up to the competitive period(s) of the year.

Progressive resistance training Strength training in which, when a set amount of work is completed, for the next session an increased resistance is applied.

Pulse rate training range The range of heart rates between which the exercise has broadly specified effects (e.g. aerobic or anaerobic).

Recovery (adequate) One-third of the period of time for the pulse rate to return to normal after exercise.

Recovery (full) The period of time for the body to return to normal after exercise.

Repetition A single performance of an exercise.

Set A group of repetitions of an exercise.

Shin splints The medical condition associated with inflammation of the boundary between the shin bone and the tissue connecting the *anterior tibialis* muscle.

Specific training Training based on the requirements of the event.

Speed endurance The ability to sustain speed running for extended periods of time.

Stage training Training in which a series of exercises is performed, in which all sets of one exercise are completed before the next is begun.

Strength The ability of a muscle or muscles to apply force.

Strength (general) All-round body strength.

Strength (specific) The strength needed specifically to perform an event.

Strength-for-weight ratio The ratio of strength divided by bodyweight to indicate the relative strength of the athlete compared to bodyweight.

Stretch reflex The muscles' natural reactive mechanism on being stretched.

Suppleness The range of movement allowed by the muscle-tendon structures.

Swiss ball Inflatable plastic ball between 40 and 60cm in diameter.

Tapering Reducing the training in preparation for a competition.

Vascularization The increase in blood capillaries found in and around muscles after most training methods.

Water-soluble Having the ability to be dissolved in water.

Year plan The plan a coach draws up of all the training to be performed during the year, organized so as to help the athlete reach a peak during competition periods.

List of Exercises

81 & 82	Kneeling single-arm raise.
83	Kneeling double-arm raise.
84 & 85	Kneeling single-arm leg raise.
86 & 87	Feet raised crunch.
88 & 89	Feet raised, arms outstretched crunch.

Chapter 6   Speed and Power Exercises

98	Bounding.
99	Sand jumping.
100, 101 & 102	Hurdle jumping.
103	Step jumping.
104, 105, 106 & 107	Discus arm/shoulder plyometric exercise.
108	Power bench press.

Chapter 7   Circuit Training Exercises

109, 100, 111, 112 & 113	Burpees.
114 & 115	Calf jumps.
116, 117, 118 & 119	Alternate leg 'V' sits.
120, 121, 122, 123 & 124	Flat twisting back hyperextensions.
125 & 126	Feet flat crunches.
127 & 128	Feet raiseds sit-ups.
129, 130 & 131	Low box jumps.
132, 133, 134, 135, 136 & 137	Standing full range body circles.
138, 139 & 140	Full narrow stance split squat jumps.
141, 142, 143, 144 & 145	Alternate reverse leg raises.
146 & 147	Free sit-ups.
148, 149, 150, 151 & 152	Kneeling rotating lean backs.
153 & 154	Lunges with full body lean.
155 & 156	Step-up sprint drives.
157, 158 & 1590	Feet raised bench dips.
160, 161, 162, 163 & 164	Sprint thrusts.
165, 166, 167 & 168	Full wide-stance split squat jumps.
169 & 170	Alternate leg raise from hip raise.
171 & 172	Double reverse leg raise.
173, 174 & 175	'V' sits.
176, 177 & 178	Elbows tucked-in press-ups.
179 & 180	Step-up drives.
182, 182, 183 & 184	Supported bounce jumps.
185 & 186	Lying abductor raises.

Chapter 8   Bodyweight Stage Training Exercises

187, 188 & 189	Squat thrusts.
190, 191 & 192	Press-ups.
193, 194 & 195	Hip raises.
196, 197, 198, 199 & 200	Free twisting sit-ups.

201, 202 & 203   Back hyperextensions.

201, 202 & 203	Back hyperextensions.
204, 205, 206, 207 & 208	Chinnies.
209, 210 & 211	Bench dips.
212, 213, 214 & 215	Full-range squat jumps.
216, 217 & 218	One leg supported squats.
219, 220, 221 & 222	Press-ups to finger tips.
223, 224 & 225	Leaning lunges.
226, 227, 228, 229 & 230	Twisting, hanging knee tucks.
231, 232 & 233	Bench back hyperextensions.
234, 235, 236, 237 & 238	Alternate leg 'V' sits.
239, 240, 241 & 242	Wide stance split squat jumps.

Chapter 9   Medicine Ball Exercises

243, 244 & 245	Squat jump vertical throw.
246, 247 & 248	Football throw-in.
249, 250 & 251	Single arm discus style throw.
252, 253 & 254	Seated throw-in.
255 & 256	Seated backward overhead throw.
257, 258 & 259	Reverse one-arm triceps throw.
260, 261 & 262	Lying vertical pushes (one- and two-arm).
263, 264 & 265	Lying throw-in.
266 & 267	Lying overhead backward throw.
268, 269 & 270	Sit-up.
271, 272 & 273	Sit-up throw-in.
274, 275, 276 & 277	Standing medicine ball circling.
278, 279 & 280	Standing horizontal rotation.
281 & 282	Medicine ball knee raise.
283 & 284	Medicine ball leg raise.
285 & 286	Medicine ball single-leg kick.
287 & 288	Medicine ball double-leg kick.

Chapter 10   Basic Strength Training Exercises

289, 290 & 291	Power clean.
292, 293, 294 & 295	Power snatch.
296, 297 & 298	Back squat.
299	Front squat.
300, 301, 302 & 303	Back squat jump.
304 & 305	Leg extension.
306, 307 & 308	Leg biccp curl.
309, 310, 311 & 312	Bench press.
313 & 314	Press behind neck.
315, 316 & 317	Arm biceps curl.
318, 319 & 320	Lat pull down (wide grip to back of shoulders).
321, 322 & 323	Lat pull down (narrow grip to chest).
324, 325 & 326	Bent over rowing (wide grip to chest).
327, 328 & 329	Bent over rowing (narrow grip to abdomen).
330, 331 & 332	Upright rowing.

Index